Cv

Text copyright © 1989 by M.T. Fish and D. Hallbery

Published by SAF (Publishing) Ltd.
P.O. Box 151,
Harrow.
Middx..
HA3 ODH
England.

Tel: (01) 904 6263

ISBN 0 946719 03 9
Second revised and enlarged edition 1989

First edition (ISBN 0 946719 01 2) 1985

A Serious Art Forms production

Printed by:The Eastern Press Ltd. Reading, Berks.

CABARET VOLTAIRE

THE ART OF THE SIXTH SENSE

by M Fish and D Hallbery

Published by SAF

F O R E W O R D

The Art of the Sixth Sense is a book about the group Cabaret Voltaire, from their early dabblings in sound experimentation through to worldwide record sales and award winning videos. Our main aim when compiling the book was, not only to cover historical background from 1973, but also to cover some of the interests and themes that have constantly been subject matter of theirs. We very much wanted to produce a book that would reflect Cabaret Voltaire's material and their personalities, rather than trying to place them into any conceived notion of how a music book should look or read.

The interviews in chapters 1 to 7 in this book were constructed from a number of interviews and conversations I had with Richard, Mal, and former group member Chris Watson in 1983 and 1984 and comprised the first edition of the book. This updated second edition features new information on the group and interviews I conducted with Richard and Mal during 1988.

Cabaret Voltaire have not always been the most public of groups or individuals, but I would like to extend my thanks to them and hope this book gives some illumination on a group who have been described as being both intriguing and infuriating.

M.T. Fish

C O N T E N T S

PUTTING ON THE PRESSURE

It might be thought possible *to obtain*

CABARET
VOLTAIRE

ASPECTS OF ASTUTE DESIGNING

PETROL OR
ELECTRIC

is it just another new Group?

C/V

laboratory-standard high fidelity modules

I'VE
HOOKED
ONTO
SOMETHING
PRETTY
GOOD

DOWN
WITH
THE NEW

Product Digest

THE OUTER LIMITS?

Project 60

Our latest
see-through
creation

How to make the smell

INTRODUCTION

It was the general spirit of the original Cabaret Voltaire, formed by a group of artists known as Dadaists in Zurich in 1916, that provided the initial impetus for Richard H. Kirk, Stephen Mallinder and Chris Watson when they first started playing around with the sounds eschewing from their tape recorders in Sheffield in 1973. Initially, what was to become the second incarnation of the name Cabaret Voltaire, was just a group of friends recording various sounds and re-enacting Dadaist type jokes with them. In the Dadaist Manifesto of around 1916, Huelsenbeck says about being a Dadaist, "Life appears as a simultaneous muddle of noises, colours and spiritual rhythms, which is taken unmodified into Dadaist art, with all the sensational screams and fevers of its reckless everyday psyche and with all its brutal reality". Kirk, Mallinder and Watson became fascinated with the ideas and spirit of Dada and began playing around with tape recorders to see how their ideas related to sound.

These ideas culminated in 1975, when the three staged their first performance of these sound experiments and assumed the name Cabaret Voltaire. The concert itself was an experiment that ended with Mallinder being taken to hospital with a chipped bone in his back and Richard flinging his guitar into the audience. Clearly the audience was not ready for sound experimentation on this level. It is perhaps easy to forget in a popular culture that moves so fast, how unacceptable within a musical format Cabaret Voltaire must have appeared at that time.

Just as Duchamp had shocked people with his found objects like urinals, displaying them as art so as to alter people's perception of them, so Cabaret Voltaire picked their own 'readymades' of everyday noises. These noises were built up on tape loops and embellished with odd instruments and voices so as to produce a dense percussive sound. The Cabaret Voltaire of 1973 to 1976 was purely involved in the manipulation of these sounds and the compilation of tapes of them. Any association within the framework of contemporary music only came later when through the live presentation of these sounds, coupled with subsequent interest in the music papers, they began to become defined as a music group.

This experimentation may have been of immediate interest to those who had delved into the writings of Burroughs or Ballard, or listened to likes of Can or the Velvet Underground, but what appeared to be the subject matter behind the material was probably enough to cultivate interest in itself. When these experiments were put to vinyl, the early titles of the records didn't mince words – 'Baader Meinhof' and 'Do the Mussolini Headkick' were indicators that were bound to lead to a certain notoriety. It appeared to be a direct immersion into a world of political violence, drug abuse and mind manipulation that made some people suspicious of their intentions.

The reason why their material became available on record was due to a non-contractual deal established with Rough Trade in 1978 – the year that saw them release their first EP. It was an often uneasy relationship that was finally to spawn 8 LPs and 5 singles. All these recordings were assembled at the group's working base in Sheffield called Western Works. In reality, this studio was a couple of rented rooms above an old Northern sweat shop where they started to build up a facility for recording and recoding their source material. Using their own studio they were not only able to establish a high level of independence but it also gave them time to cultivate their own brand of sound and visual presentation.

By 1981 the output of Cabaret Voltaire had become increasingly musical and it is perhaps not surprising that Chris Watson, the least musically orientated of the three, left to pursue a career as a sound engineer for Tyne Tees Television at the end of that year. Although the group had obviously lost an important contributor to their material, the two remaining members decided to continue as a duo – supplementing their recordings and live performances with other musicians where necessary. Either coincidentally, or partially as a result of Watson's departure, there appeared a significant shift in attitude towards the distribution and production of their material. After 8 years as pioneers of independently-minded music, the time seemed right for them to step out of the shadows in an attempt to allay complacency and to reach a wider audience. The result was a recording deal with Virgin through Stevo's Some Bizzare label, and for the first time the group attempted to shake off the gloomy, introspective image they had now attracted. Around the same time they set up, in conjunction with Paul Smith, their own video and record label called Doublevision. Initially the label concentrated on video releases - the progression into video being a natural one for Cabaret Voltaire as they had always put a considerable emphasis on a visual accompaniment to their live shows. The advent of commercial video gave them an opportunity to co-ordinate the visual and sound aspects of their work.

The Cabaret Voltaire of 1978 through to 1984 produced music and videos that presented the world as a mesh of disjointed imagery and incessant rhythms, rejecting both storylines and song structures. Their sound was a dense mass of instrumentation, whilst visually they threw up an apparently unfathomable collage of images which refused to concentrate on isolated topics. They somehow managed to be arresting and amusing, whilst managing to avoid the pained efforts of those whose aim is merely to shock or repulse.

Cabaret Voltaire had no approach as such, they used a blanket of religion, violence, obsessions and mysteries and linked them with an atmosphere within the music that leaned toward tribal ceremony or religious invocation. As a method of presentation it was far from a contrived examination, but one which relied on the random and spontaneous. It was strictly apolitical, amoral and unopinionated. Whether they were too concerned with offering any explanation as to what their manipulation of the cut-up technique was revealing is uncertain. The material certainly begged questions about some

9

fairly strong issues, such as paranormality and the power of violence and fanaticism within society. What they appear to have attempted was to produce a soundtrack to accompany people's obsessions with these topics.

Taking such an unopinionated approach was obviously open to criticisms of being either nihilistic or just plain naive. After all it is very easy to knock other people's standpoint when you give none yourself. However, the group appeared genuine in not trying to let their opinions as individuals get in the way – simply laying open some avenues for people to explore themselves. Whether people were able to gain anything tangible from Cabaret Voltaire's blanket presentation might go part of the way to explaining the difficulty they were to encounter later in trying to crossover to a more mainstream market.

So, does this beg the question, "Was it just one big con?" Did they just have a couple of lucky breaks, conning their way to a certain notoriety by throwing together a few ambiguous images and menacing song titles. Or was it really an effective use of a cut-up technique that used a thought provoking language which was not always easy to understand, but did get to the heart of some basic motivations. The truth if it be known probably lay somewhere between the two.

What is certain is that their presentation had nothing to do with a direct sense of realism. It was a sense of surrealism that was at odds in an '80s environment which saw many TV programmers and record companies settling for the lowest common denominator, steering clear of things that didn't wave their intentions like banners. This 'safeness' is probably best exemplified by the promotional video, where a total distrust of anything that wasn't in a certain mould, made most of them nothing more than predictable adverts.

Cabaret Voltaire, on the other hand, were strongly rooted in a surrealist tradition – a tradition that has always been involved in the manipulation of the everyday through the subconscious and out into the bizarre and humorous – rather than presenting the world as it would seem. (Although some people, then and now, did find it difficult to see the humorous side!)

Some of their most successful extrapolations were during their rare but often anticipated live performances. During a performance an audience could be assaulted with a barrage of rhythm interspersed with taped voices and an onslaught of cut-up imagery. The images were built up from a wide variety of TV clips, particularly from news bulletins of rioting, images of Nazi power, military devastation and humiliation. These were interspersed with the group's home made videos often shot at various locations where the group had toured, featuring flashes of hand-held camera work down the Reeperbahn or through the congestion of central Tokyo. Other clips had the two, often clad all in leather, prowling around derelict sites or riding in taxis.

A common criticism of Cabaret Voltaire was that they concentrated on the bleak, darker areas of life. They have often been described as cold, grey and gloomy. It is true that they may have been rather unfairly grouped together with the mass of doom-laden sixth form poetry merchants that appeared in the wake of Punk, but nonetheless it was an image that they were to find hard to shake.

So, ultimately behind the curtain of cut-ups are Richard and Mal – 'The Cabs', both serious and mischievous, both personable and polite. Their happy-go-lucky attitude had set them apart from the pretensions of 'rock' musicians, or the cosy, insular cliqueiness of jazz or the avant garde, or the secular elitism of the independent scene. Cabaret Voltaire were to find themselves plunged into a grey area between the three, caught in the throes of commerciality versus creativity – an area that was to close up and become less of a comfortable place to sit as time went on.

Musically, it is probably fair to say that their true potential was realised in their early recordings. Latterly they have become more and more closely allied to other contemporary groups and sounds, ultimately to be overtaken by a mainstream that was ready to capitalise on the ground that had been broken for them by the likes of Cabaret Voltaire.

It is always difficult to assess any one group's influence in an area such as contemporary music. However, if nothing else, Cabaret Voltaire (along with the now defunct Throbbing Gristle) were, if only briefly, responsible for pioneering the acceptability of many sounds that would not have been considered anything to do with music in 1973. Particularly the inclusion of snippets of 'found voices' that has always been a trademark of their material. They also seem to have responsible for inspiring a number of groups who continue to work on the fringes of the music business and whose primary aims appear to be to widen the boundaries of 'music'. To this end Cabaret Voltaire were instrumental in defining a strand of popular music which came to be known as experimental or 'industrial', but now whose heyday has surely passed and whose practitioners Cabaret Voltaire have moved on to leave far behind them.

The interviews in the first chapters of this book were conducted in 1983/4 and attempted to isolate some of the subjects and strands that have run through their material as well as covering historical background. The interviews in chapters 8 and 9 were conducted during 1988 and as such have their own introduction – serving as a coda to a career which has spanned 15 years from the production of a limited edition cassette to worldwide record sales.

from
naked
meals
to
record
deals

- EARLY YEARS

- INITIAL INFLUENCES

- EARLY CONCERTS AND TAPES

- EDINBURGH ARTS PACKAGE

- ROUGH TRADE

Was the initial idea to be a music group?

Richard: I suppose that depends, on how you define 'music'. No,, the initial idea was to be more of a sound group, just putting sounds together like jigsaw pieces. If the end result did sound like music then it was purely coincidental.

Mal: It started off purely as an area of interest – in the sense that it was something we all felt we wanted to do. We had always been interested in literature, art and music, but sound was the way we developed– not as music specifically, but using sound in general.

Why do you think you chose to develop in sound and not other areas – film or photography for example?

17

Mal: Well, photography is very much an individual activity, there's nothing corporate about it. Film making is similar perhaps – but as far as we were concerned at that stage, they both lacked the advantage of immediate feedback. With sound you can get an immediate idea of what you are doing by listening to the interrelation of the ideas you are trying. With photography or film you have to wait – just literally having to wait until they are developed. With sound we had the automatic feedback from the use of the tape recorder, which meant we were able to hear the interrelation of the things working immediately. The only other thing that might have been available in the visual media was video – but the immediacy of that was not available to us at that time.

Also, a lot of it was tied up with the fact that we didn't want to involve ourselves in the snobbery associated with many of these other artistic areas. We didn't see ourselves as actors – we didn't want to go on stage in that sense. Music in general has a lack of snobbery. Popular music specifically, is very much a working class culture. No matter how much it has been manipulated by big business, it is still a working class culture.

Richard: Although we concentrated on sound, I had always been interested in film. I bought a standard 8 projector a long time ago, and while I was at Art School I used to make collages.

Was the initial idea spontaneous, or did you have a definite idea of what you wanted to do with the sound you were generating?

Mal: No, we didn't have a definite idea – initially it was just audio masturbation, it was just having fun with tape recorders.

Richard: It was just three friends with common interests – we didn't take it that seriously. For instance, before we even played live, we would drive around playing tape loops out the back of a van, or just turn up in pubs and just turn on the tape recorder for the hell of it.

Mal: We literally went up to Chris's loft two days a week and just messed around. It was still just the idea of tackling boredom and of actually feeling that you were doing something rather than just going out and getting pissed. We felt we needed to exorcise some sort of spirit, some sort of devil that was there.

I know Chris Watson was a telephone engineer, what were you and Richard doing at that time?

Mal: When we first started I was betwe en school and college. I had just taken a year off and was labouring at the time.

Richard: I was at school.

Did you first become friends at school?

Richard: No, we met literally on the streets, just hanging around the city centre. Mal and I were skinheads.

Could you name any people in particular that directly influenced what you were producing at that time?

Mal: There were certain points and influences I can see with hindsight that triggered it off. I think Eno in a lot of ways was quite an influence, in the way that he used a tape recorder on the first Roxy Music LP. It was the things that he was doing with tape – and as we had access to tape recorders – the whole idea of messing around with a tape loop became interesting.

Richard: I wouldn't say it was the way that Eno approached sound that influenced me so much, it was more the fact that here was someone who was making music but actually making the point that he was not a musician. At that time most people thought that if you were going to make music you had to learn to play an instrument. Here was someone who was saying that anyone could do it – just give it a go!

There were no other influences I could name specifically, other than the odd thing we might have picked up on in an interview – for instance, Eno might might have mentioned the name of a German band that sounded interesting, so we would try and find out more about them.

Mal: I think we grew into it, rather then having a reservoir of influences behind us. We didn't start off with that sort of reservoir of ideas filtering through from people like Can, John Cage, Stockhausen or whoever. It started off in very purist terms – it was just a very simple thing, the idea of messing about with a tape recorder. It was only as we developed that we picked up on people

The early Cabaret Voltaire - Kirk, Mallinder, Watson - Dadaists 60 years on.

like Can, Velvet Underground, Burroughs, or Kraftwerk, and seeing how they related to what we were doing.

What instrumentation did you have at that time?

Richard: When we first started we didn't have a synthesiser, Chris and I both had tape recorders and we had an oscillator that Chris had built, along with some odd percussion.

Mal: I think that Chris approached it from a technical as well as an artistic standpoint. Because he was a telephone engineer, he was interested in sound as a technical source as well as an artistic one. Richard and I provided more of the artistic link to it in some ways, but the whole germ of it was very spontaneous. When I think about it now I still don't know why we started to do it. I think it was out of pure boredom more than anything else.

The next step in terms of instrumentation was when we went up to the Music Department of Sheffield University where we had access to a VCS 3 synthesiser and a Revox. Obviously that appealed to us because Eno used a VCS 3 – however, the idea of using a very technical synthesiser rather than a keyboard based one was also very appealing to us. Those were the only instruments we had access to.

So, when did you first start to acquire instruments?

Mal: As I've said we started working in Chris's loft with only tape recorders and a few things to bang as percussion. However, the first instrument we bought was an AKS, which was a suitcase synthesiser – again it was a non-musician type of synthesiser, more of a sound generator. I suppose the next thing that was an indicator as to the way we would develop, was that Richard bought a clarinet for about £15. The a few months later, it was Richard's birthday and Chris bought him a guitar for £5.

Richard: Looking back, I think the conscious decision to include electric guitar was quite significant. It didn't matter so much whether you played it or hit it with sticks, it was the fact that we could draw on a whole new sound source, and that gave us more scope.

Mal: At the time we bought these instruments, we saw them as just a way of generating a noise to relate to the things we could generate using tape recorders and Chris's oscillator.

What about rhythm? How did you achieve a rhythm, or was it simply a case of using anything that made a noise?

Mal: The whole rhythmic side of things came about from banging anything that was around the loft at that time – pure percussion. Whatever sounded good, you hit it. Also we used a lot of tape loops, and although not percussive in themselves, the whole notion of the tape loop is based on repetition, and it therefore becomes a percussive pulse.

Leading on from that, as another way of generating rhythm we bought a drum machine. What appealed to us was the idea of providing a faultless beat, a pulse behind what we were doing to link things together. We didn't really want to use a drummer at that time because we didn't want to be part of the 'rock music' tradition. In a lot of ways we wanted to parody that whole 'rock' tradition and integrate it into the basic idea of sound collage. We wanted to juxtapose different forms of music, such as the avant garde experimental tradition, with a parody of rock music. However, it is only really now in retrospect I can see that those were important formative things in the way we developed.

You mentioned your early recordings were purely for your own benefit but obviously your attitude must have changed at some stage. Why was that?

Mal: Well, after a while we realised we had hours and hours of stuff and we thought it was pointless just doing it, it must be to some end. The first thing we did was to start compiling a tape of some of the things, sifting through to find the best stuff. When we had the master tape, we prepared a cassette of which we did a limited edition of 25, which we duplicated one to one. We packaged it with a Xeroxed sleeve, a track listing and some photos – then basically we just started sending them to people. Eno was one of the first people to get one of the tapes, because at the time he seemed to be a kindred spirit. He was more interesting to us than any of the avant garde musicians we could have been associated with, because he was doing something interesting whilst still within a 'rock' field.

"We began to feel the need to express ourselves beyond the confines of Chris's loft." Mallinder

I think we realised that, although we still had an independent mind, by compiling a cassette we were starting to make ourselves accessible in more traditional ways – although we did not want to let this change what we did, or the way in which we presented it.

Around that time you put together a package for the Edinburgh Arts Festival. How did that come about?

Richard: It was through some people who were involved with the Department of Music at Sheffield University, but I can't remember how they got in touch with us. They used to put on performances, and they must have heard of us and asked us to do something as part of some things that they were taking up to the Arts Festival. We put a 50 minute package together for them. Unfortunately, at that time I was going to Europe, so we never actually went up to Edinburgh to appear. We never got it back either!

What did the package contain?

Mal: We did a 50 minute piece of tape that was cut-up and linked with a drum machine and sporadic pieces of sequencer. There was also a film to go with it, as well as an inflammatory type of hand out. The hand out was also a cut-up, the idea of which came from Duchamp more than anyone else – we weren't Burroughs influenced people at that time. We did it literally in the Dadaist way, we took the pieces out of a hat and Xeroxed them off.

You say that the hand out was inflammatory. Was the idea of it to shock?

Mal: Yes, it was literally to shock people. One of the lines was, "Murder the Angolan bastards that killed Colonel Callan", which was quite provocative at the time.

Would you say that this constituted a political input to your material?

Mal: Yes, but we felt divorced from it. Although it was inflammatory we also felt we were taking the piss out of artists in some ways, as well as being artists ourselves. That gave us the right to be inflammatory. We believed in our naive way, then and now, that the artist can be inflammatory and remain divorced from his actions.

Did you think the package might change people's opinions?

Mal: Yes we were naive enough to believe that. We never thought we would become famous, but we thought for one brief moment we might become notorious.

You were obviously becoming increasingly confident about presenting your music and material.

Mal: Yes, I think we were coming out of our shell. We didn't have much respect for most of the people we associated with – like the Music Society of Sheffield University. We began to feel the need to express ourselves beyond the confines of Chris's loft.

Richard: I think it was because there were very few people doing anything like what we were doing outside of the very avant garde scene. There was nothing else going on, everything else seemed very safe to us – there was nothing that interested us, except for a few German bands and a few odd things we had heard. We were trying to work within a 'rock' framework because there was more of a potential audience. We obviously couldn't continue to play to people at the Department of Music at the University, otherwise nobody would hear us!

So you had the idea that you might expand from just experimenting in Chris's loft. How did that actually come about?

Richard: The first gig we ever played, some bloke said to Chris, "You've got a band, what sort of stuff do you play?" Chris told him that we played a bit of rock, a bit of everything, which of course was a total lie but at least we got our foot in the doorway.

Mal: This was around the time when the band was expected to play two sets in between the disco. We also played a school in Bury which was arranged through the Music Society. We were beginning to realise the potential, it was far more anarchic playing live, seeing those germs of ideas that had gone onto tape coming to fruition live.

What was the audience's reaction?

Mal: People really hated us. However, a lot of friends of ours would come along just for the laugh, and a lot of them were nutters, so nobody really dared do anything. Often the people who were our friends were a lot heavier than any potential trouble makers.

So, initially was playing live more just for a laugh, or did it add to what you'd put on tape?

Mal: On the one hand it was literally for a laugh. We did it for fun, however perverse that fun might have been. On the other hand it was done within a serious mode of wanting to create. However, we weren't serious about it in the sense of wanting to make it into a career, it was done with the idea of, "Let's go out and shock people". It wouldn't shock people now, but it did then. What we did then was like what a lot of other groups are doing now – only in 1975 people's outlooks and links with music were very different.

So, what were the next steps after those initial concerts and the tape?

Mal: By the end of 1976 the punk explosion had started and there was a very early fanzine in Sheffield called Gunrubber, it appeared about the same time as London's Sniffing Glue. Gunrubber was run by Adi Newton (later to form Clock DVA) but it was mainly his sidekick Paul Bower who picked up on us, he thought the whole idea of us was hilarious. He knew of us from years back – because for some time we had become fairly notorious figures in Sheffield.

Why was that?

Mal: Because as well as being into music we were also into fashion. We used to buy all our clothes in London, wear all the Teddy Boy gear etc. I think the whole idea of us intrigued people. We had looked rather peculiar stemming back to the early Roxy period – and I think people thought that we must be doing something interesting because we looked so odd.

Were you ever physically intimidated because you looked so odd?

Mal: No, not really, because there were loads of us and we all used to be drunk half the time. It was mock bravado similar to the old adage, "If you can't fight then wear a big hat". So, we didn't get intimidated that much, but people were wary of us. Also, we knew our limits, we wouldn't go down the East end of Sheffield and go into the pubs dressed like we were, but we would go to the

"In those days we never asked to play dates, we never pushed ourselves, people asked us to do it." Kirk

"Although we were thought of as one of the pioneer independent bands, we were still not entirely happy on Rough Trade." Mallinder

University and some of the clubs. In those places we were looked on as weird characters – it was safe but it was also funny to intimidate people – not physically, but by our looks.

I think that was what was interesting to people like Paul Bower. We had brought out this weird tape that more people had talked about than actually heard. At that stage our mystique was larger than ourselves – rather like the early Residents. It was that whole mystique that Gunrubber picked up on – and so they did an article about us. We played a couple of times with this reputation built up around us, so even though people thought we were absolutely crap, there was still this air of mystique.

So you were fairly notorious around Sheffield. What led to that notoriety spreading further afield?

Richard: There were two things that led to us getting our name around outside of Sheffield. Firstly, I sent a cassette to Jon Savage, who was then working for Sounds, and two days later I got a letter saying that he wanted to come up and do an interview with us which led to the first article about us in the music papers.

Secondly, I also sent a cassette to New Hormones, who had released the first Buzzcocks EP, and Richard Boone (The Buzzcocks' manager) was really into it. Word got around with a few people in Manchester, and that led to us being asked to play the first Factory club. In those days we never asked to play dates – we never pushed ourselves, people always came and asked us to do it. We've never really had to sell ourselves.

I think also, that the things we cited as influences helped, maybe you could call it namedropping. I think there were a lot of people in England who were into The Velvet Underground, Kraftwerk, Can and other German groups, but there was no other group in England putting that sort of thing together at that time. I think the word got round that someone in England was working along those lines.

How did this increase in interest in the group culminate in the recording deal with Rough Trade?

Mal: Jon Savage was really the person who got us the Rough Trade deal, because he was the person who persuaded Geoff Travis to come and see us supporting The Buzzcocks at the Lyceum.

28

Richard: I think also Genesis P-Orridge had a lot to do with it. We wrote to them at Industrial and sent them a tape. Originally they wanted to bring it out on the Industrial label but they didn't have enough money. In the end it took a year for the Rough Trade deal to happen, before we actually went down to London to meet them.

What was it like playing The Lyceum at the height of the punk era?

Richard: It was really quite scary, because in the past we had only played infront of about 100 people, apart from the time where we had played for about 400 people at the school in Bury. At The Lyceum it was also the first time we'd played infront of an audience who hadn't come specifically to see us – and there we were playing infront of a load of thrashing punks.

Mal: The gig itself was horrendous. The only good thing about it was that we went on first and people weren't as drunk as they were later on. At first, we thought we had got it bad, we got spat on and had glasses and bottles thrown at us, but later when The Buzzcocks came on, they had an iron bar thrown at them as well – and it was them everyone had come to see! So we reckoned we hadn't come out of it too badly. Needless to say, the sound was abysmal – it was quite funny looking back on it.

What were your personal reactions to punk? All of a sudden a whole load of groups appeared who were trying to be provocative.

Mal: Yes, shock became a wholesale industry.

Did that make you want to do something different?

Mal: Well, it did and it didn't. The whole spirit of punk was fine and some of the music was too. In the initial stages at least, you were getting people saying that it was really different and breaking down barriers, and to some extent it did. It was only later that it collapsed in on itself and became a stereotype like any other – like rock 'n' roll, for example.

Richard: Although I liked a lot of the punk music, I always felt that a lot of it was not looking forward. To me a lot of it sounded like The Rolling Stones, who I had always been into anyway. I thought

Geoff Travis
Rough Trade
202 Kensington Park Road
LONDON   W11

Dear Geoff

        :CABARET VOLTAIRE:

TG/IR informed us you might be able to help us
in getting an EP out.

All Our material is recorded and stored on
master reel/reel tapes (a domestic 2 ch, 2 Tk).
This is adequate.

We copy onto cassettes for convenience.

I am awaiting the delivery of a Revox B77 H/S
from which we can supply edited master tapes
at 15 i.p.s.

Any advice/help would be gratefully received.

                    Yours sincerely

                    CR. Watson

                    C.R. Watson
                    for CABARET VOLTAIRE

Dear Cabaret Voltaire,

thanks for your letter.I've been being near to contact with you for a
long time.What has stopped me ahs been our lack of money.Yes I would
very much like to help you to put an E.P. out.Can you please send
me a cassette of what you would like to relese and I will give it
a listen and then we can talk about what will be the best way
about going to release the record.
You remember that I talked to you after your Lyceum experience and I sai
-d r then that I was interested.I am still so.Please let's speed ourselv
-es up so that we can produce something very good very soon.

Thanks agin for making contact.I saw Genesis P. today and we talked a l
little about you,he saying that you might be playing together in
Wakefield.

best regards,

Geoff Travis.   Geoff Travis

30

we were saying similar things to the punk bands, but hoping to do something a little different in terms of what we actually produced.

Do you think that it actually changed what you were doing?

Richard: Yes, obviously there were influences. I think our music became a little bit more guitar-based. However, that kind of influence had been there anyway from The Velvet Underground with that kind of scratching wall of guitars.

How much do you think that you were a part of punk?

Mal: We were swept up with the momentum of the whole thing – but it was very much a movement of the moment – so we utilised it for the time being. We played gigs because we were asked to play – just carrying on because we fitted in somewhere. We were left to our own devices, but we still fitted in.

We didn't think about where we would progress to from there, because the whole climate was totally different then. Now, we have a climate where people tend to think in the long term. Maybe, it's media pressure, but we tend to be in this situation of not thinking about the moment because the future is upon us.

So, what were your attitudes at the time of getting the Rough Trade deal. How committed were you?

Mal: Very committed, because we had taken so much time getting to that situation. We thought, no matter how subconsciously, that someone was going to latch on to what we were doing and at some stage we would be in a position where we could spend more time doing it. I don't think I ever thought that I would be doing this for the rest of my life, but I thought at some stage we would be able to concentrate on it full time – whether it would be for one or two years or whatever.

When did you first start recording at Western Works?

Mal: I think it was just after the Lyceum gig as I can remember rehearsing for that gig in Chris's loft. But we recorded the first EP at Western Works on a Revox we had bought about that time, having toyed with the idea of hiring one. We thought that Revox was the ultimate thing to have at that time.

With all the independent labels just starting up then, I suppose it was an ideal time for you to get a record deal.

Richard: Yes. Mind you, we had tried all the major record companies by sending cassettes to them.

Did you get any response at all?

Richard: Well, we always got letters back, I've still got them all. I've actually got one from Simon Draper who was then just an A&R man for Virgin records – ironic in view of what has happened since.

If at any time a major record company had come along and offered you a deal, do you think you would have signed?

Mal: If the situation had arisen, I think to be honest we would have done. Although we were thought of as one of the pioneer independent groups, we were still not entirely at home on Rough Trade – so if a major had come along we would have seriously considered it.

So, what was the set-up with Rough Trade?

Mal: Initially when they approached us they said that they weren't a label but a licensing agency. They had already licensed 'Mister Basie' by Augustus Pablo, and they were just about to licence the Metal Urbain single. So, initially they were just a distribution set-up that dealt with weirder sorts of records. By the time they approached us, they suggested that they would like to release a record, but that we would have to wait 6 months until they had enough money. Later that summer they got in touch with us and said it was financially OK. So we recorded the tape, went down and cut it, did the artwork ourselves, and Rough Trade released it – and that was it. In fact we were their first British release.

At what stage during your relationship with Rough Trade did you become self-financing?

Richard: It wasn't until 1979, just after the first LP 'Mix Up' came out. We got our first royalty cheque for £4,000. I had been kicked off the dole anyway, so it was quite fortunate for me that the album

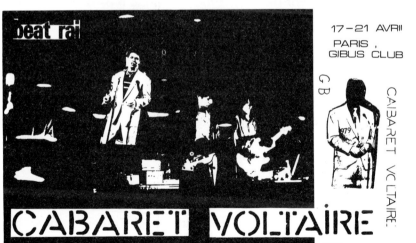

The Cabs play a week in Paris.

came out at that time. The money we got from the first single was negligible really, only a couple of hundred pounds.

Were there any other labels interested in you at that time?

Mal: We had done a couple of tracks for the Factory sampler, and at that time we weren't too sure what was going to happen next. We wanted to do an album and both Factory and Rough Trade were interested in bringing it out. Basically, Rough Trade came up with the money first. I think that was probably a good thing – in a lot of ways we would probably have been too much the ideal Factory band.

Factory work very much on a corporate identity whilst Rough Trade tend to have the identity of championing the independent group. Do you think that was a weakness?

Mal: That was Rough Trade's weakness in the sense that they wanted to be all things to all people. They tended towards being an enormous amorphous blob, drawing too much in, rather than concentrating on a few things that they actually wanted to do. I think they were scared in case anything escaped the net.

Factory, on the other hand, were more selective working on the Bauhaus principle of the same producer, same type of artwork for all their bands.

In some respects wasn't Rough Trade the ideal label for you, because they let you get on with your own thing and all you had to do was supply them with the tapes and they would release them?

Richard: Yes, it was an ideal situation in some ways – and that is probably the reason why we decided to change it – because it was too safe. The whole process of making an album at Western Works, sending Rough Trade the tapes, the album selling X amount but never any more, became unsatisfactory.

Were you disappointed with Rough Trade?

Mal: Well, we never really fitted in with Rough Trade – it got to the stage where the only contact we had with them was sending them the tapes, and them bringing the albums out. We had never wanted to be part of that Rough Trade scene – that whole Bohemian 'Ladbroke Grove scene' – pseudo-intellectual and pseudo-ethnic.

Richard: Rough Trade at that time seemed to be going downhill. I think one day we just realised that we hated most of the groups on the label – and we began to question why we were on the label at all. They did have their ups and downs, mind you, and they did try and get a bit more organised later on.

Mal: I think they hated us because we remained in Sheffield, and they were very much into this commune type thing. A part of that was their idea of seeing other parts of the record business – i.e. "You're on Rough Trade, we bring out your records and you work behind the counter selling records in the shop." We didn't give a fuck about that. We said, "We're not selling fucking records". We were also the ones who wanted better sleeves – we wanted things done classily, we have never gone for the sloppy hippyish extreme.

As well as sleeves and presentation, do you think Rough Trade short-changed you in terms of advertising and promotion?

Richard: Yes, they never really went for that, and they still don't. It got to the stage where we were in Sheffield, and they were in London with the whole clique that was The Raincoats and Scritti Politti. We began to find out that these bands were being supported by Rough Trade, but they weren't actually selling any records. We were making two albums a year and they were making one every two years and still getting the money for it. That really pissed us off when we found out about that.

A lot of people internally at Rough Trade fought against that – I'm not going to mention any names, but it resulted in the sacking of some people. At this time there was also an attempt to reorganise the whole set-up and become more business-like.

Were you playing a lot of gigs at that point in time?

Mal: We were doing them sporadically. We were starting to play abroad – we did a week at the Gibus club in Paris. The main turning point in terms of performance was when we were supposed to do the Rough Trade tour with The Raincoats and Kleenex. The day before the tour Chris suddenly said that he didn't want to do it. I was quite pissed off at the time because I thought it would be a good way of learning, despite the fact that it was a very traditional way of selling ourselves. In retrospect, I'm really glad we didn't. The prospect of going out on the road with a bunch like that didn't appeal to me.

I think pulling out of the tour was one of the best things we did, because it stated our independence. Of course, it really annoyed Rough Trade – to the point where, apart from Peter Walmsley, everyone hated us. However, it did prove to them that we weren't going to toe the line.

Richard: Apart from that, we didn't particularly like what any of the groups involved in the tour were saying – particularly the feminist thing, we felt rather out of place amongst all that.

So, you didn't particularly identify with the Rough Trade image. What about Cabaret Voltaire's image? It seems to me that there were times during your early career when you could have been described as the New Wave's answer to Hawkwind. Were you worried about comparisons like that?

Mal: No, because with us there was always a certain amount of personality coming through. People related Cabaret Voltaire to me, Chris and Richard. With Hawkwind the stage show was a lot of fuzz guitars and a load of hair, whereas we had our personalties coming through. I think the Hawkwind reference is valid – but I don't think we were ever as cosmic as that!

AUGUST 1981

CABARET VOLTAIRE : RED MECCA (ROUGH 27) PRESS INFORMATION
- -

The three members of CABARET VOLTAIRE began working together as a
group in the mid-seventies, putting together a multiplicity of taped
sounds, voices, excerpts of 'found' music, around which they constructed sound effects from synthesisers, treated guitar effects, drum
machine, and a variety of wind instruments.
A limited number of cassettes of this music were made available,
(and have since been released on Industrial Records cassettes,
The Early Years 1974 - 6), and the band played some live dates
which were not exactly received as a new form of popular art.
In 1978 the band had releases on two of the new indepedent labels,
Factory (the Factory sampler EP, a double EP with four bands), and
their first Rough Trade release, the four track Extended Play.
Their relationship with both these labels enabled them to perform
more frequently, and they played with bands such as Siouxsie & the
Banshees, The Buzzcocks, Joy Division during this period, although
they concentrated more on further recordings at their four track
studio, the Western Works in Sheffield. The result of this work was
a further single release, Nag Nag Nag (RT018), which established their
popularity more strongly, and their first album, Mix Up, a synthesis
of early and then current work, which was released in late 1979.
Infrequent live performers, the band recorded one of their performances
in London, at the YMCA series of concerts in 1980, and decided that
the material should be released, but as a 'budget' album. In conjunction
with Rough Trade, this was done and the album was released soon after.
(Cabaret Voltaire, Live at the YMCA, Rough7).
The band members had been consistently working on improving their
studio during this period, and were continually recording new material.
A further single, Silent Command (RT035), and the unusual 12", Three
Mantras, two tracks of more than twenty minutes each side, were the
recorded evidence of this period of work, and then, in mid 1980, their
most thoughtfully constructed recording work to date, The Voice of
America (Rough 11), was released.
This period represented, to date, the most consistent working period
for the band and their collaborators at Rough Trade. Concerts in
Europe and America were arranged for them, and the album was set for
release in variuos European countries, America, Australia and Japan.

Press release for the group's Red Mecca LP. Chris Watson was to
leave the group in November 1981. (Contd over)

2

1981 has seen the band extending their working schedule and repertoire
to include work on video projects, mostly in conjunction with
Factory Records, work on a film soundtrack, Johnny Yes No (commissioned
by the BBC), individual production work with some bands from their
area, (for example, Eric Random, They Must Be Russians, & 23 Skidoo),
the development of further studio space, and the introduction of an
eight track machine into their studio.

At the same time the band have continued to release a variety of
recorded material in different forms, in an attempt to reflect
their differing tastes and techniques. This year has seen the
release on the Belgian Crepuscule label of three tracks, mainly
recorded in America, a solo cassette by Richard Kirk, (on Industrial
Records), the cassette only release of their last London concert
in February (Rough Tapes, Copy002), which has been in the indepednent
album charts since its release six weeks ago, and now, in August,
their new album RED MECCA.

RED MECCA is an album of entirely new material, recorded on the new
eight track equipment now installed at the Western Works. For the
band it represents a significant new venture in their recorded sound
and in the 'emotional texture' of the music. As with their earlier
material, the album is a coherent whole, and their will be no singles
from the album etc....

The album is being released in Europe, America, Japan and Australia
in September, and the band are planning dates in Germany and
America for October.

Two singles and a 12" edited version of the film soundtrack are
already recorded and will be released by the end of the year.

For all further information please contact either :
Chris Williams or Peter Walmsley at Rough Trade on 01 221 1100.

chris
watson

If we could start by talking about your decision to leave Cabaret Voltaire and go and work for Tyne Tees Television. How did the offer of the job come about?

Chris: I came up to Newcastle for an exhibition of recording equipment and I met up with a few people who I had made acquaintance with previously. I was aware of some of the things that Tyne Tees were doing and someone at the exhibition suggested that I ought to get in touch with them – so I did. From there I went up for an interview and they offered me a job virtually immediately – the following day I think it was.

Were you thinking of leaving the group at that time or did the offer of a job prompt you to leave?

Chris: It wasn't a deliberate decision of mine to say that I must leave the group and find another job. The job offer came up and I thought about it for some considerable time. I decided, after talking to Richard, Mal and Margaret (Chris's girlfriend, now his wife), that I would like to do it.

Richard said that it appeared to him that you weren't enjoying being in the group as much as you had in the early days.

Chris: Yes, the job seemed to come at a time when it appealed to me more than being in Cabaret Voltaire. I don't look at it as a right or wrong decision – I still think about it a lot.

At the time you left the group they were becoming more musical, were you becoming more distant from that?

Chris: No, not necessarily. It was a mutual interest in the way that the group was going. We were all interested in the non-musical side initially – but that was my main contribution throughout my time with the group. My contribution was not through a particular instrument as it was with the other two – Richard with the guitar and wind instruments, and Mal with the bass, percussion and voice. I was more concerned with sounds generally and in the production of the records. I worked more as an engineer of the sounds rather than actually playing an instrument to produce them.

So, were you the one who provided most of the 'found' material?

Chris: We all did it, but as I say, I tended to do more of it than the others because I have never had any interest in actually playing an instrument.

But you were credited as playing organ on a lot of the tracks?

Chris: Oh yes, I was. That was really through force of circumstance. I played organ in order to go out and actually reproduce some of the stuff that we did live – which we had made a conscious decision to do early on. The fact that I had used a keyboard with one of the synthesisers I used to have, meant that I said I would work the keyboards, so I ended up playing them.

However, I very quickly lost interest in keyboard synthesisers so I bought a very old Vox Continental organ which was quite superb – I fell in love with the sound and the look of it. It was red with reversed black on white keys, it just looked superb. I got interested in actually trying to create a rhythm with that. The only keyboard player I've ever had any respect for or been interested in the technique of, is Irmin Schmidt of Can. He seemed to use the keyboard in an interesting way that hadn't been explored by anyone else.

What about Eno?

Chris: Oh certainly. Early Roxy Music for us was probably one of the sparks for the group. I remember seeing them in early 1972 at a college in Sheffield. I was completely knocked out, it actually changed my aspect on virtually everything I did regarding music – both listening and production. I was interested in Brian Eno's technique and some of the sounds he produced. I learnt a lot about contemporary music through that, whereas my interest before that had come more from the classic avant garde such as Stockhausen, Schaeffer, Satie, and people like that.

Any other influences you could mention?

Chris: The greatest influence of all was learning, reading about and reliving the period of Dada. Seeing various films, exhibitions, shows, listening to old recordings. That was my initial inspiration to actually do something.

You mention film, what was your input to the visual side of Cabaret Voltaire?

Chris: My practical part in the construction of the films was very small, as was Mal's. It was mainly Richard, although the decisions of what to use and what not to use were fairly democratic. As jobs in the group became allocated that became one of Richard's roles. He had experience of film at Art College and he was interested in the application of it – he also had a certain amount of equipment initially. He has gone on from there with his interest in video.

43

"The only keyboard player I've ever had any respect for is Irmin
Schmidt of Can." Watson

Talking of roles, it appears to me that Richard has absorbed more of your role in Cabaret Voltaire more than Mal has.

Chris: I always worked very closely with Richard, because a lot of our interests outside the group were very similar. It goes back again to the connection with Dada – the films, publications and literature.

Would you say that Mal's interests were slightly different?

Chris: No, not really. I would just say that Richard's and my interests seemed to be closer because we had a closer working experience. Richard and I worked on a few basic things together before Mal actually joined the group, although we knew him then. I don't know if you went that far back with them, but there were times when there were six or seven people in the group that became Cabaret Voltaire. This goes back to going around to people's houses in the evening and going into pubs and playing tape loops – there was quite a crowd of us at that time.

Anyone you could mention that has moved on to anything of note?

Chris: No, not anyone that was connected with the group – but around at the time were people like the Human League who we were in close contact with. They weren't actually connected with us but a lot of the interests were similar and we would talk about things in pubs etc.

Would you go as far as to say there was a Sheffield scene at the time?

Chris: No, I wouldn't say that at all. It was just people getting together and talking about things that they were interested in. I'm sure it's happening now in every major town or city in the country. There was no way you could call it anything more than that. It was just people going out and enjoying themselves, getting in touch through parties – a lot of contacts were made through parties, just good fun.

What was your attitude toward playing live, was that a side of the group you liked less?

Chris: No, I thoroughly enjoyed it as a physical experience. It was incredible, it was like nothing else I have ever done. It was enjoyable providing you didn't do too much of it. We were never a touring band, that wasn't something we were interested in.

However, I did find when we travelled as Cabaret Voltaire that there was a feeling of empathy when we did gigs. We always met people whose views and opinions were so close to our own without ever having made prior contact with them. Abroad in particular, where people have been brought up in different ways yet arrived at a similar point. There was definitely a feeling of international comradeship if you like – various links of communication between groups of people who didn't know they could communicate. It was a certain feeling that was utterly incredible – to talk to these people and realise that you are of a similar opinion. It gave us great heart at the time and a stronger belief in what we were doing. We felt generally we were on the right lines.

Returning to the records, have you got a favourite track by Cabaret Voltaire?

Chris: I haven't really, no.

Have you a least favourite track?

Chris: No, not really, there is nothing that sticks out because you are so closely involved when you are recording. I still play some of the things, they sound very raw, that is one of the things that I am still very pleased about.

Was that rawness purely down to the lack of technology and equipment?

Chris: Yes, but also because of the spontaneity, we weren't actually going for quality or clarity.

Certainly Cabaret Voltaire have moved towards both clarity and quality since your departure. What is your opinion of their material now?

Chris: I like it, I think it sounds great.

Could you envisage yourself fitting in with the more disco-orientated material if you had still been in the group?

Chris: I don't know. They are doing so many different things. The disco material is only a part of what they do. On that basis I would say yes to the question, but obviously if I had still been in the group I would have had some influence on the output, otherwise there would have been no point in me being in the group in the first place.

Could you envisage any future collaboration with Richard and Mal?

Chris: Yes, I would love to. I still keep in touch with them quite regularly, fortunately we still seem to have kept reasonably good friends, as we were primarily before the group. I would love to work with them again, I could never establish a similar working attitude with anyone else.

Are you worried about being forever labelled 'ex Cabaret Voltaire'?

Chris: I think it is inevitable to a certain extent, what with people's attitudes. There is no point in being worried about it, it is bound to happen. I don't regard it as detrimental, I'm proud of some of the stuff I did.

You haven't totally given up recording. Could you outline how your project under the name of The Hafler Trio came about?

Chris: Since leaving both Sheffield and Richard and Mal, and moving to Newcastle, I became aware of what I was missing. After the initial period of coming to live in a different city and working for someone else again, I realised I was missing both Richard and Mal as friends who I had known for years, but I was also missing them as working partners. As I said before I don't think I could ever establish the relationship we had between the three of us with anyone else. I could never work with a group of people as closely as I worked with Richard and Mal. I also missed working in the field of recording and producing something, and working toward future projects – be they records or whatever.

I became aware of someone who supported us at a concert Cabaret Voltaire did in Newcastle years ago. They got in touch with me through the seeds of information process. We talked and we found we had similar interests in a few areas – quite a few areas in fact – and that he had been interested in certain things that I had been thinking about. Anyway, the upshot of it was that we actually got together and started recording material for no other purpose than to satisfy our own desire to do it – which was remarkably close to the initial intention of Cabaret Voltaire. The result of which is the LP, "Bang" – An Open Letter. The material was collected over a number of years, using some old material and some which was recorded specifically for the record. It embodies a lot of what I wanted to do while I was with Cabaret Voltaire, and also things I have thought about since I left Richard and Mal – and now have actually been able to put down on tape. It has ultimately been quite satisfying in a selfish way.

Are there any other activities that you have been involved in, or anything that you particularly want to do in the future?

Chris: I have also done one or two things for radio – a 45 minute documentary and one or two other pieces – which have been fascinating to produce and great fun to make. I see them all in a way as a continuation of my work with Cabaret Voltaire, because I still have the same feelings about it as I had then. A passion for certain subjects that have carried through. It is something that I have found I have got to do, because I believe very strongly in it, and I enjoy doing it basically.

So, I hope to produce a number of things ranging from general natural history subjects right through to various sound processes. I am trying to avoid the use of the word 'music', because that is something that has gone down and down hill as far as I am concerned. I am losing interest in it all the time, which is very sad. It is not a conscious decision to do so, but I am more and more appalled by what I hear. I am feeling more and more drawn toward natural sounds of every description. I have been listening to one or two live concerts on Radio 3 which are mainly classical music, but some are what they call avant garde as well. I'm more and more drawn to a live sound produced by a single pair of microphones to record specific subjects.

I have had some contact with, and use of, the Carl Reich Sound Field Microphone and I am interested in that field, in the use of ambiosonics and peripheral sound sources, and live recordings of things in general. Recently I have been interested in ritual music, the use of chanting, again attached to my old interest in rhythms and repetition which was very strong in Cabaret Voltaire. Again, not as music but in pure sound and dynamics, ambience and timbre.

I know some of the pure sounds that interest you most are those made by birds. How long have you been interested in ornithology?

Chris: I am not actually interested in ornithology, that impression has come about because of my initial interest a few years ago in the recording of natural history sounds. Some of the most accessible and easy from a recording point of view come from birds, as well as being the most interesting natural sounds. So, it was necessary to acquire some working knowledge of ornithology in order to record these sounds and achieve some level of success. The good terrorist ethic of 'knowing your subject'. So, in that respect ornithology was a secondary interest brought about by my interests in natural history recording, something I have continued to do. In fact, something I have continued to do a lot more of, as I find it more and more an abiding passion. It is something I enjoy tremendously, actually being in the middle of a wood at midnight, or four o'clock in the morning, with a pair of gun microphones – sat underneath a bush or secreted away somewhere, listening over a pair of headphones to sounds that are so different that they really defy description in the proper sense. It is almost like you are listening in to another world completely, a world which has an atmosphere and mystery about it which I find completely fascinating. The physical sounds themselves I find quite stimulating because they are like nothing else I have ever heard. Particularly as over the last couple of years I have become less and less interested in music.

What about video. What is your opinion of it?

Chris: Video is a huge question – obviously tied up with broadcasting, television and the media in general – unless you look at it purely as a technical instrument or tool. It will continue to develop technically, but I don't know if it will become more available to people. Certainly the price of it has probably bottomed out I would guess. It is quite a late comer into, for want of a better phrase, 'the music industry'. Video production is one of the major sources of material for TV broadcasting – but what I'm particularly involved with is post production regarding the sound. The facilities for that are increasing rapidly at the moment, and have done over the past year, which only serves to increase the power of the medium. A medium which can be used or abused depending on whose hands it is in. I also believe that video has rather limiting problems and dimensions that are not constrictions when using film. I believe film is generally a more powerful instrument and something I am more interested in at the moment. Having had experience with video I quickly got saturated with it. As with anything else, as soon as the music industry got hold of it as a promotional tool, a lot of the techniques were bastardised and therefore a lot of the power has gone out of it.

Finally, have The Hafler Trio got any plans for live presentation?

Chris: Not in a conventional stage presentation – I'm not interested in that side of it anymore at all. We have got some ideas about short films that might go along to exhibitions or shows of some description.

The Hafler Trio
Sound Recordings
Robot (U.K.)

generation
of
the
beat

- CONSTUCTION OF MATERIAL

- WORKING WITHIN THE MUSIC
  BUSINESS

- GOALS AND MORALS

- ART AND POLITICS

If we could start by talking about the musical side of your activities. How would you describe your method and approach to the construction of your music. Has it always been a case of putting a percussion track down and then constructing all the sounds over that?

Richard: Yes, I would say that is probably true 75% of the time – at least these days anyway. Come to think about it, it always has been. Sometimes we might start with a voice tape or a tape loop and we would construct something around that. For instance, on the LP 'Microphonies' I used a tape that I found which had me, Mal and Chris talking to this American bloke three or four years ago. So I cut it up, stuck it onto tape and put it on one of the tracks. Doing things

53

like that appeals to me, it goes back to the Duchamp principle of a 'found object'.

Mal: A lot of the times we would try not to consciously use rhythm but try to be aware of it in a non-percussive way. We would nearly always start off with a basic track that would run all the way through to give a whitewash or a background. In a lot of ways it was like a soundscape. I think as we progressed we tended to concentrate more and more on rhythm.

Richard: I see it rather like building up a painting, sticking the background down and then adding stuff on top of that. There is no difference really, that is exactly the way I would approach doing a painting.

Mal: As we build it up we tend to know what clicks and then we embellish those ideas. Sometimes we have a set idea and sometimes we just mess about and see what happens. Often it's a case of building things up to lose them later because they have become superfluous.

Does the lyric always come last?

Mal: No, that is not strictly true – particularly of late. Often the vocal will go down two thirds of the way through. Sometimes I find it hard to work purely to a rhythm, so I may wait until there is a simple musical thing for me to feed off. Often once the vocals are on we put more stuff on top – but as soon as the track has some bare bones I start working on the vocals.

How has the way that you fit the vocals within the lack of a conventional song structure changed since the early days?

Mal: Initially I was more of a traditionalist, I saw lyrics fitting in with musical structures, whereas Richard saw them as cut-up prose which would be totally juxtaposed to the music, a sort of poetry on top of sound. In the early days I didn't write many of the lyrics, Richard wrote more and I played more. Nowadays the roles have become more clearly defined and polarised. I took on more of the lyrics as I became increasingly conscious of the way the words fitted into the way our music developed.

"We were interested in the voice as a rhythm, using it as just
another instrument rather than straight singing." Mallinder

THE ART OF THE SIXTH SENSE

So, initially you used the voice more like another instrument?

Mal: Yes, exactly. We were interested in the voice as a rhythm, using it as just another instrument rather than straight singing. Certainly, using a song structure of verse/chorus/verse wouldn't work for us because we would lose a bit of the feel and the spontaneity.

The lyrical subject matter is sometimes very obtuse and indirect – not the same as the sort of insular lyric a rock group might produce.

Richard: I don't see anything particularly bad in rock lyrics – because the people who write those sort of lyrics produce a lot of good music. That is because they think of themselves as producing rock music, whereas I see what we are doing as something other than that. I suppose you could say that we were Jacks-of-all-trades and masters of none.

Is provocation still an important side to your music, or is the accent on dance-orientated material more important to you now?

Mal: We are still a bit of a paradox because people tend to class us as some sort of new dance group now – but no one at our performances ever seems to dance much. We are the dance group that no one ever dances to.

I think the provocative element has diminished over the years, mainly because people's idea of what is provocative has been eaten away. There was that whole period during the punk explosion of 1977 to 1979 where shock value was being sold wholesale. Today you would have to make a really determined effort to go out and shock people, and we don't particularly want to do that now because it would dismiss the other ninety percent of what we do.

Do you think that there are a lot of people who are disappointed that you are not as provocative as you were in the beginning?

Mal: Yes, there probably are. It is easy for them to say that, they don't have to do it themselves. It is like you have been given this role in life – you are the provocateur and you have got to do that. They don't take into account that at some time you might want to do something more subtle.

If we provoked at the time, it was because we hit a nerve, maybe we don't hit a nerve anymore. The Sex Pistols wouldn't be the slightest bit provocative if you put them in the context of today. The point is that they were provocative at the time. Now, you just get John Lydon still playing 'Anarchy in the UK', acting like a real wanker, thinking he's still being provocative.

Richard: I don't see much point in being controversial just for the sake of it. I just don't like the idea of retreading old ground, and that is why we try to keep moving on all the time.

What do you think of your old material now?

Richard: Every now and then I dig out some of the old tracks and give them a listen. I think it is a good idea to do that. I would stand by everything we have ever done personally. With all the stuff, there must have been a good reason for doing it at the time and that is good enough for me. I don't know whether Mal would agree with that.

Mal: I don't listen to our old stuff very often, in fact I rarely listen to our music at all. When I do listen, it is with a mixture of pleasure and embarrassment – embarrassed in the sense of growing up in public.

In general, as regards listening to music, I can home in on things that have a certain amount of spirit, but are also listenable to. What we were doing with some of the early stuff was producing something that was interesting, but in a lot of ways totally unlistenable to. In those days the ideas were more important than the end result, but we always believed that the end result would catch up with the ideas.

In particular, a lot of people say that they think 'Three Mantras' is unlistenable to. Would you say that it was your least favourite Cabaret Voltaire record?

Mal: No, it is not my least favourite. In fact, I loved it because it was a record that stuck out in people's minds. It was the record that people couldn't work out why the fuck we did it. For that reason it is probably the most valid record we have ever done.

The fact that there were only two tracks on the record was obviously a joke (this was lost on one reviewer who reviewed it as three tracks) - also the length of the tracks seemed rather extreme for what they were.

Mal: It was a joke in that sense as well. It was attempt to push things to their extremities. I don't think we would do it again.

Do you think you are inflexible about the length of your tracks. There almost seems to be a standard length to a lot of them these days?

Mal: I think that is a valid point. I think some of our tracks are too long – then again some of them are too short! We still work on feel more than anything else as regards the length of our tracks.

Do you think that because the newer material is more music orientated that it might become dated a lot quicker than your older material?

Mal: That's true, but it is not so much the way we have developed, but more the way the link between music and technology has developed – which has tended to stereotype certain sounds. Before the mass availability of sequencers and drum machines it was very polarised – you had guitar and drum based music, and you had electronic music. This situation still exists now to a degree, but there are people like us and New Order who are making the crossover. However, a lot of records now have drum machine and bass sequencer on them, so the technology tends to become the common link.

You use of drum machine and bass sequencer has inevitably meant that your material has tended towards a disco sound. Do you think that an LP like 'The Crackdown', for example, was successful at being a disco album with a difference?

Mal: Yes I think it was. My only qualms with that album was that it came out a bit late. It lost something to me because it took so long in coming out. I never thought it was going to be an album that would last forever, but I still stand by it.

Richard: I think that album was successful because it got us across to more people than we normally would have done. We virtually doubled the record sales and therefore doubled the number of people we could communicate with. It meant that our music got

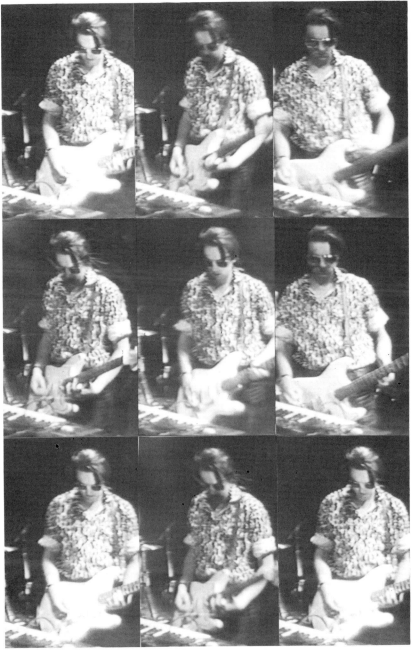

Stills of Richard from a 1983 TV appearance on The Switch.

played a lot more in clubs, and it got in the bottom end of the charts which certainly helps in terms of getting noticed.

You obviously try quite hard to keep up with the ever advancing technology in recording techniques and instruments. How do you choose the instruments you use?

Mal: We haven't got that many new instruments, actually. Most of the equipment we have bought has been studio recording equipment. We still only have two synthesisers and one of those is six years old. Other than that we tend to hire them in when we need them, use them on a couple of tracks and then send them back. If we had bought them we would feel obliged to use them on all of the tracks, but by hiring you don't have that obligation. We soon get to know which ones are good for certain sounds.

Do you not have a problem trying to work with some of the more complicated drum machines and sequencers that are available to you?

Mal: Yes, with something like a Fairlight, for instance, you have to rely on the expertise of an engineer. They are so expensive to hire that you couldn't contemplate doing it all yourself because it would take three times as long.

What would you say to people that say that Cabaret Voltaire was based on one idea and you are only using increased technology to say the same thing?

Richard: I would go along with that. Mind you, I think the one idea was a very good one! I think it is the same with most bands – they generally have one slow piece and one fast piece and just do variations on those two themes. As long as you can keep people interested enough to want to buy it, I don't see anything wrong with that. I think the same is true of most film-makers.

How do you see your music developing?

Richard: In the format that the music is in at the moment, I don't see us as doing it for years and years, although I think we have got a few more albums worth yet. However, in the future I still think we shall continue with music, but it will probably tie in more and more with the film aspect. This will mean it will probably be more abstract and atmospheric in nature. Soundtrack work is something we would like to push for. When we sign a new publishing deal we would like it put in the contract that they look for soundtrack work for us. It is one of the functions that a publisher should serve.

On the whole I think our music will become more schizophrenic. I think the music on our records will become more accessible, but on the other side of the coin, we will retain the facility for producing soundtrack music. I think it is a more effective for us to work that way. That is what I like about the way we operate, we always try to keep it open-ended so we can go off into any area without it being too contrived.

When you say the music will become more accessible, do you think that could stretch to a top ten hit?

Richard: Yes, I think that would be really good.

Mal: But we wouldn't lose any sleep if we didn't get one.

Richard: The main advantage of one would be that it would put us in a more powerful position. You tend to command more respect out of the whole industry, and if we were to do a film we would be able to go and ask for £50,000 and get away with it.

'Just Fascination' was probably the closest you've had to a hit single to date. Did the fact that you used a producer on the remix of that make the difference. Will you continue to use producers?

Mal: Yes, we will for the singles – but with an album it is hard for us to work with a producer because we are so used to working on our own. With a single it is a bit different because you are drafting in someone else's expertise on the subtleties of what a single is. It is quite nice to learn from someone else in that context, in the way that we did from John Luongo on the 'Just Fascination' single, for example.

Richard: It is quite nice to let someone else loose on your material, but it is not something I would like to see happen all the time. I'm too personally involved with it to allow someone else's grubby fingers all over it. I feel too close to what I do. It is sometimes difficult for us working in a studio in London, because we have to work through an engineer, as opposed to when we engineer it ourselves.

But a good producer is necessary for a single though?

Richard: I think a single is an artform unto itself. There is nothing better than a good single, is there? Although I'm not sure about what people like Trevor Horn get up to. It seems so contrived. I don't know how contrived the pop singles of the past were, but it does seem that the innocence, naivety and freshness are missing a lot of the time these days.

But even in the past there was a heavy reliance on the producer. George Martin, Andrew Loog Oldham for instance.

Richard: Obviously these people are important and have a role to play.

Do you think there are any advantages to not ever having had a hit single?

Mal: Yes there are. A disadvantage with a hit single is that you gain a millstone around your neck. However, it would be good to have a top seller because it might get the record company off our backs.

Would you say that you were moving further and further into the 'music business'?

Mal: Yes, but the further we move into it the more we find ourselves going off at tangents. It is alright as long as you accept it as a mechanism that you want to use rather then become a part of.

Richard: I think in our case, the more successful we get, the more freedom it is going to allow us. We'll be able to turn round and tell people to piss off!

Mal: Maybe I have just become more cynical about the whole business since we started. It would be nice to remain fresh and naive, but to get out of it what you want, you have to be realistic.

I think we reached a crossroads a few years ago and we had to make a decision. We had achieved a certain amount but we felt we had reached a plateau. Although in some respects it would have been nice to retain a level of obscurity, after a while that was beginning to lose its appeal. We could quite easily have found ourselves washed up. As with The Residents, the obscurity principle reaches a certain stage, and after that people turn round and say, "Well, who gives a fuck anyway". You can only remain mysterious for so long, eventually you can just end up on the side sad faced.

Would you say that in the independent ethic is becoming more and more redundant, and you might as well go straight for the widest possible coverage?

Richard: Yes, provided that you can retain control of everything that you do – which is still the case with us up to now. Nobody can force us to do anything we don't want to, like taking loads of singles off one album, for example. They cannot market any of our product, in any way, without our consent – we have to be consulted about everything. That would be the only way that we would enter into anything of that nature now, especially dealing with a major record label.

Do you think that you would have held out for those principles if a major label had been interested in the early days?

Richard: Probably, who can say? We were a lot more naive in those days. We have learnt a lot more now about the pro's and con's which gives you a standpoint with which to fight against them.

However, you think you are in a good position now in terms of controlling what you do?

Richard: Yes, I think even now we can do exactly what we want. Although I'm only just starting to realise what makes half this business tick, and what things you need to do to reach a wider audience. For instance, in retrospect it was a mistake to make 'Just Fascination' a double A side, because as 'Just Fascination' was the A side of the 7", 'Crackdown' was ignored. We learnt through experience that if you release what you think is a good value record with two A sides, one of them will get ignored. Now I would say release them separately, even though that has gone against what we have said in the past.

Why bother ?

Britain is going **DISCRETE**

Many people are quite unnecessarily **funny**

2

je descends pour « ep
me une dernière fois jusl
; filmer. Le 15 septembre
une soupe d'algues mortes
qui remuait les sédiments,
r. Marc Jasinski, le camer
ir mauvais temps, ciel co
lmer nos trouvailles. Le c
vavant nous envoyer un c

CABARET
VOLTAIRE

oojamaflip

Do you think that Chris Watson leaving the group influenced your decision to take a further step into the limelight?

Mal: I don't know really. To Chris's credit I don't think he was interested in that side of it much. It is difficult to analyse anything like that in hindsight.

But could you see yourselves as doing the same sort of music as you are doing now if Chris were still in the group?

Richard: Well, yes and no. I don't think the question is particularly relevant because it seemed to me that he just wasn't enjoying it anymore. He always said that if he wasn't enjoying it he would stop. He never saw himself as doing it for the rest of his life. Mind you, neither do I!

What do you see yourself as doing then?

Richard: Living a life of luxury!

Financed by?

Richard: Ah, there is the rub!

So, you don't see yourself like Jagger – still on stage at 45?

Richard: No I don't. Mind you, he's probably a lot fitter at 45 than I am now! I still respect them because they are a fairly controversial bunch, even now.

So, have you never really thought about what you do in terms of a career – but very much taken things as they come?

Mal: I think it is all wrapped up in the way that we like to approach what we do. Some people working in our area have very specific goals, which they either achieve or fall short of. We have never put ourselves in that situation, because we have never actually defined what we want to achieve. Therefore, we never have to worry about falling short of goals because we don't know what they are. We try not to blinker ourselves. We fell into music, we fell into films and video, so I suppose in a lot of ways you could say we were complete upstarts.

Although you say that you have a lack of direct goals, there is still a general impression that you know what you are doing.

Mal: Yes, I think that goes back to us working by instinct rather than having a direct message. I think we live in a world where instincts are very important because of the pressures of situations around you. I think the whole idea of being totally in control of your destiny, or even feeling that you are, is totally false. This maybe an existentialist point of view, but I do think there is a danger in being disappointed with not achieving something.

When I say that we don't set ourselves goals, it doesn't mean that there aren't certain standards that we try to achieve. I think the amount you learn on the way is a hell of a lot more useful than achieving goals. Christ, I'm making it sound like the Olympic Games – competing is greater than winning!

Would you say that you would extend that philosophy of not setting goals to your personal life?

Mal: Yes, I think I do really, although I do have aspirations. It is difficult not to sound hypocritical about this, because on the one hand I am saying that I don't have any specific goals, while on the other hand I have to have aspirations. It is a paradox, but I think as long as those aspirations are not too clearly defined, then they are OK.

Similarly, would you say that your amoral attitude to your material extends into your personal philosophy, or do you have a set of morals which dictates things that are acceptable to you?

Mal: Yes, I do think I have a set of morals. There is an amorality about our material, but there is morality in our personalities which possibly tempers the whole thing. Obviously I have got morals - but then again my morals must be quite flexible because I'm not exactly sure what they are!

There must be some morality. I think it is all a case of dignity, the whole idea of not shitting on somebody. For instance, I thought Jock Macdonald making a record with the bloke who broke into The Queen's bedroom was totally immoral. It's not that I give a shit about The Queen, but it is unfortunate that we are at a time when

Mal with Bass. "The trouble with an ordinary guitar is that the strings are too close together."

people can do that sort of thing and make money out of it. This might seem an old fashioned viewpoint, but I couldn't be totally Machiavellian or opportunist like that. So, although I'm in it for myself, it's not to the extent of downgrading other people or stooping below certain standards or levels. It is all about dignity – even if what I've done really sucks, at least I will have done it in a way I would be proud of.

Richard: I suppose I must be moral somewhere. I mean, I disagree with violence and exploitation, but I am a firm believer in individualism and doing things for yourself. Maybe it is a crude attitude to take, but I think if you have got something to say, and you are determined enough, then there is a way to get through and do it.

But there is a thin line between encouraging individualism and arriving at the position of allowing an 'anything goes' policy which can lead to exploitation.

Richard: Well, what do you do? It's a bit of a horrible world we live in – so do you just say, "Fuck it", and just look out for yourself, or do you try and change it. I still don't know which is the best attitude to adopt. I probably use a mixture of both.

A lot of musicians, Paul Weller or Elvis Costello for example, take the change the world attitude and get involved in promoting their politics and political parties.

Richard: I don't like that kind of sloganeering. Mind you, I think we are more political than any of those people, purely because what we are advocating is individualism. This might sound like a sort of anarchy – it is very difficult to explain – I think we are political but not overtly so.

Mal: Personally I think the whole thing of political preaching really sucks. There again I can't really knock anyone for doing it if they do feel motivated in that way, and do feel that personal responsibility. Personally, I can't see myself using whatever position I am in to toe any party line because I don't believe in any party line. However, I am sure that a person like Paul Weller, much of a tit I think he is, sincerely believes that he is helping by taking that personal responsibility to push people along a certain line. I find that whole aspect a bit frightening in the fact that people do take notice of his position and what he says, and that people are stupid enough to change their politics by what pop group they like.

One area that a lot of musicians traditionally get involved with is that of nuclear disarmament and CND. What are your opinions on nuclear issues?

Richard: That is one thing I'm not too sure about. Obviously there are lots of different arguments you can put forward, but nuclear arms are a reality and they are not going to go away overnight. The superpowers are not going to destroy all their nuclear weapons because there is no trust between them.

Mal: The thing that frightens me most about nuclear weapons isn't America or Russia, it's the Third World. God help us when the Arabs or the African states start lobbing nuclear warheads at each other, because they are getting the technology.

I find it interesting because in a lot of respects the threat of nuclear weapons is just playing on people's obsession with death – which we are all subject to. However, it doesn't affect my day to day living particularly. Basically, again it is almost an existentialist thing. Whatever I might think or however much I hate them it isn't going to change the situation. I think CND sells crap to people just as much as the government does.

Richard: Yes, I have never supported CND, I don't think that is a way to go about getting things done. No one takes the slightest bit of notice of peaceful protest, it has been proved many times before. People only take notice of violent protest. That is why I admire some of the European peace movements more. In Germany, for instance they get really heavy – which is a contradiction in some ways for a peace movement – but at least they stand a chance of getting things done.

Are you saying that some violence is justifiable?

Richard: It is never justifiable, but it is something that is there, and it often works.

So, are you a pacifist then?

Richard: I hate the word pacifist, I don't like what it smacks of. I prefer the word humanitarian.

By using some political material do you think that people are going to inevitably label you one way or the other?

Richard: Yes, I suppose so. For instance, I remember when the first EP was released with 'Do the Mussolini Headkick' on it, a lot of people thought we were a bunch of fascists, while a lot of others thought we were punks. I remember getting collared around that time by some National Front people in Leeds.

So you don't think artists should get directly involved in politics, what about when politics gets involved with art?

Mal: That is where we in Britain are starting to play a very dangerous game – where standards are going to fall because the politics are coming first. This is why you are getting all these Channel 4 programmes made by people who haven't got a clue about making a TV programme or a film. However, because their intentions or attitudes are such, then they get it shown. Conversely, you have a whole generation who have something to contribute, but because it doesn't toe the line they never get a opportunity to present it – which is really sad. It ends up where you get the situation of a load of left wing Oxford graduates making programmes about steel workers when they don't know the first thing about it.

Richard: Obviously everyone's taste is different in terms of what is good and what is not – but I think generally I would agree with that. I remember going to a meeting about Cable TV and Cable stations and ending up walking out. The whole thing was a pile of shit, programmes about the community, the oppressed, all that sort of stuff. People don't want to see that, they should be talking about making things that are worthwhile and interesting to watch. Also, they are very suspicious of you if you don't belong to an organisation, 'somebody against the something or another'. It's the same with these government bodies that give out arts grants – if you go along as an individual they think you are an out and out fascist.

You have already stressed that you don't want to preach at people, but how important is it for you to influence what other people think?

Mal: It is important for us to make people think, and thus I suppose influence them. However, I also find it quite sad that people take influences quite literally, in some respects all we have done is clone a number of Cabaret Voltaire type bands and people. It's just part of human nature.

Richard: It was much the same with punk and The Sex Pistols, although I'm not saying it was on such a wide scale with us. It's a case of seeing something and latching onto it. I'd say we take the basic underlying point of an influence and use it to do something, but not doing a carbon copy. It's OK to be influenced by something, but that doesn't mean you have to do something that sounds or looks exactly the same.

You could take the attitude that people get what they deserve. It is down to way that people are educated, I think the people are educated in the wrong way. I don't think that people are encouraged enough to think along their own lines and act in a way that they think is right. I think there is something radically wrong with the whole education system – it just isn't working, from the day you start school to the day you leave.

So, what would you say your influence on people was?

Richard: I don't know, it's difficult for me to say. I mean, you tell me what our influence is. I think the one thing that people do miss about us is our sense of humour. I mean, everything we do is definitely not deadly serious.

At times you have encouraged others by helping to record and produce their material.

Mal: Yes we have done, but I'm drawing back a little bit from that now. It was becoming very easy to slip into a village-minded attitude, collecting like-minded people around you and helping them. I'm probably not doing that as much as before, because I was

Richard sports 'Cabs mac' on the cover of NME, Nov 1980.

tending to lose perspective, and I felt I was becoming a bit of a parody of myself. I was beginning to think that it was the way that Cabaret Voltaire should act, and I was doing it because of that. So, I felt the need to back off a little bit, not in an aloof or elitist way, but just keeping my distance.

Richard: In terms of people using Western Works, it got a bit ridiculous. It wasn't a commercial studio and we had our own things to do. We couldn't play engineers to every local band that came along because we wouldn't have had a chance to develop ourselves.

Also, it is difficult to work in a production capacity for another group – in some respects if you are asked to do so, you should be given a free rein, otherwise what is the point of having you there at all? I'm very wary about working with other people in that capacity, because some people are never satisfied and are always wanting to change things. I just haven't got the time to go along with something like that.

Do you see yourselves, along with people like The Human League, ABC, Clock DVA and Heaven 17, as having promoted a music scene in Sheffield?

Richard: No, not particularly. I can see that people might look at us and think that here were a few people from Sheffield who have gone out and done something – made a few records. We have never gone around preaching to people, telling them to form a group and then we would give them a hand. I think the 'Sheffield music scene' is a bit of a myth anyway – there has never been that many venues or platforms for expression here.

Particularly in the early days, Cabaret Voltaire tended to be portrayed as having a rather gloomy image. Are people disappointed when they meet you and find that you aren't gloomy introspective types?

Mal: A lot of people are disappointed, I don't know why. Mind you the ones who are, tend to be boring depressing people themselves.

Groups like New Order and The Fall would seem to suffer from the same thing. You once told me that they were two groups that you most felt an affinity with?

73

Richard: I was lying! No, it probably was true at the time, but I'm not so sure now.

Mal: I still see parallels between us and New Order, because they are also regarded as long mac, philosophical, almost Kafka types. We both still have that stigma.

New Order seem to play up to that image, especially in interviews, whereas you approach them with a more straight forward attitude.

Mal: Well, that is because they don't like doing interviews and they would rather let the music speak for itself. As a group they don't like coming out with blanket statements. The fact is that some groups look good in the press and others don't. For instance, Echo and the Bunnymen talk in phrases that look good in the press – they are a media group. New Order don't talk in those phrases and I don't see why they should. The point is that they are interesting people but they can't pin-point what they do in a few sentences.

You on the other hand, always seem to be very honest in all your interviews, you never play those coy games.

Mal: Yes, we are. Maybe that is why we have lost our appeal to some people. Perhaps a lot of people who originally liked us, went off us, because there was a mystique built up around us which disappeared when they realised we were real human beings. I think maybe we shouldn't have been real human beings!

Maybe a few temperamental tantrums in the press would have helped?

Mal: Yes, I suppose that's it. We are just ordinary working class Northern people and perhaps we should have hidden it better.

So, do you think you are typical Yorkshiremen?

Richard: I should bloody well hope not!

a
contemplation
of
dangerous
games

- PORNOGRAPHY

- DRUGS

- CENSORSHIP

- TV VIOLENCE

- NAZI IMAGERY

If we could talk for a while about some of the things that are censored or banned for public consumption in this country. It must raise a problem of h ᶜ*ar you can go with the images you choose for your videos and subject matter for your music. For instance, you have used clips of pornography in your visuals, why?*

Mal: Actually, pornography doesn't matter that much to me. The way I see our use of it, is as a way of spitting back at censorship as much as anything else. Richard is a better person to ask, maybe it's my Catholic upbringing!

Richard: I think pornography is very powerful imagery in much the same way as Nazi symbolism. Also, it is something that society has

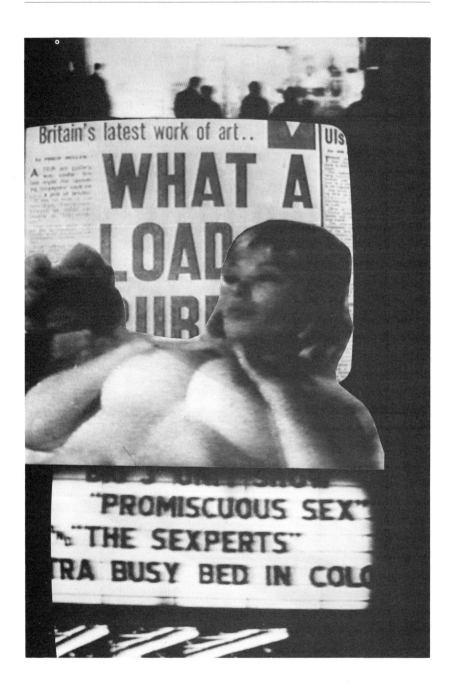

ruled as being taboo. For that reason it is something that I go for straight away – even now it gets people's backs up.

What do you think would happen if there were no censorship?

Richard: In terms of pornography, I think people would lose interest in it. The whole taboo stems from when you are a kid and you are told that nudity is not the done thing – people are not supposed to see you naked. It's just another example of society's tricks to keep you in your place.

Mal: I don't think the situation would change much from what it is at present. However, there is so much money made out of pornography, I don't think it is in a lot of people's interest to stop censorship. If it did stop, I think it would be like water finding its own level, it would be the same with drugs and licensing laws. I can't envisage a whole society motivated by pornography.

Richard: In the case of drugs, a lot of people equate them directly with crime, but the reason why they go hand in hand is the fact that they are illegal, and therefore a lot of people who get involved are really nasty pieces of work. Most of the crime comes from the buying and selling of drugs, and not the effect that the drug itself has on people.

So, what is your attitude toward the use of drugs?

Mal: I think a lot of people still believe in the old hippy ethic of searching for something, which is quite interesting in some ways, but doesn't mean anything to me personally. Basically I would rather read about that sort of thing in books like Aldous Huxley's 'Doors Of Perception', because it is a lot safer, and a whole lot cheaper!

I think people take drugs for three main reasons. The first I have already mentioned – those people who are looking for something, whereby it is another form of religion, just another crutch to lean on. The second are those people who are totally screwed up, in which case they are the wrong people to be taking drugs. Thirdly there are those who take them for purely hedonistic reasons, which would be the reason I would take them. I think it one of those stages you go through in life.

Richard: I think it very much depends on the type of drug you are talking about. A lot of people do take them purely for pleasure, whilst others take them for the way it alters the state of mind. In terms of LSD, and to a lesser extent marijuana, it is seen as a means of achieving a trance-like state, and as a means to a vision.

This trance-like state, or vision, is what Huxley defined as 'suchness' – or seeing objects in a different light. Do you think there is anything in that concept, or would you tend toward the view of the people who say that drugs are a limiter to perception?

Richard: Well, I think there is something to be said for both schools of thought. Personally, I would tend toward Huxley's viewpoint. For example, anyone who has ever taken acid is unlikely to see the world in the same light as they did before. To a lesser extent the same is true of marijuana. I think there is definitely something in seeing things out of context like Huxley did.

So, do you think that within that context drugs can be a useful artistic tool?

Richard: Yes, I think there is more to it than pure hedonism. Obviously it is down to personal interpretation. Even down to the use of alcohol – would Kerouac have been such a good writer if he hadn't been a drunk?

People have used stimulants of one sort or another for a very long time. They have been used in religious ceremonies for centuries. The old Shamans and healers would always get wrecked before a ceremony. I see little difference between that and a load of musicians doing the same thing! It's just another ritual procedure.

I think the important point to stress is that drugs are fine as long as you use them, and you don't let them use you. The most dangerous of all in that respect is heroin. I have never taken it myself, but I have seen enough people who have, and read enough about it to know that it is something I wouldn't want to get involved in.

Mal: I think you have to be specific about certain drugs, in that certain people can use them to the right ends, but they are very few – most people would tend to get side-tracked.

Do you think that censorship is over excessive in Britain, for instance in the case of licensing laws?

Richard: In the case of licensing laws you only have to look at Europe as a whole, where you can buy a drink any time of the day or night and there doesn't seem to be any more people drunk. In England, because you have only three hours to get blotto you go at it full pace, whereas in Europe you can take your time.

Do you think that censorship restrictions have anything to do with the fact that Britain seemingly produces a larger share of musicians working in a similar vein to you?

Mal: I don't know whether Britain does, or whether it is just that we have the channels for it to come out. I think it would be to easy to say it was due to the way censorship confines people.

However, it is still the case that you could count the number of notable French rock groups on one hand, for instance.

Mal: More like one finger! I think you have to look back and see the way the particular cultures and societies have developed. The French are a very leisure-based people in a lot of ways, whereas in Britain we still have this 19th Century work ethic which carries through society. I mean you can't name many British philosophers, whereas philosophy is a very strong French thing. Those sorts of traditions are steeped a long way back, but I don't know why it manifests itself in Britain in terms of contemporary music.

There are more outlets for contemporary music in Britain, perhaps?

Mal: Yes, people do tend to tailor their expression to the way they can get their material the best exposure.

In tackling taboos and censored subjects, do you think there is a danger in becoming obsessed with the darker side of life?

Richard: I suppose concentrating on those areas is a kind of obsession. It's something that I find very interesting, constantly delving and researching more and more about it. I suppose that you could say that it was obsessive to be interested in taboos – rather than gardening or something like that!

Mal: I think it is a criticism that could be laid at a lot of people's doors – many people concentrate on the obsessive chic of certain things. Personally I am very wary of that sort of thing. I think it is to our benefit that we are a lot more rational than some. I mean, no criticism of Psychic TV, but Gen has always run that thin line where there is a possibility of opening up something where he would have no control of the end result.

Might people then argue that Cabaret Voltaire are just a watered down version of a group like Psychic TV?

Mal: Yes, to a degree that might be true – we have the same general interest areas as Psychic TV, so people are bound to see parallel trends. I think the big difference between us is the language we use. We use the language of music and film without particularly knowing what we are trying to say, whereas with Psychic TV the most important thing is what they are trying to say, a message.

One of the largest general interest areas would appear to be the notion of control.

Richard: I think it was Burroughs who said that the machine had gone out of control. I think that is true to a certain extent in that the people who are in so-called control don't know what they are in control of anymore.

Mal: Yes, control is sometimes manifest and sometimes subliminal and subconscious. I think when you analyse it, the whole notion of control is actually an internal thing – it is within you, you are the one who is conscious of the control. Control is a thing of your own mind and the only way to liberate yourself from it is to liberate your own mind.

But how can you liberate yourself from those aspects of control that work on a subconscious level?

Mal: I don't think you can. I think the only way is to try and become more aware of it, to become more knowledgeable – although in some respects the more you know the worse it becomes. I don't think you can shut yourself off from it. I think you are a participant whatever happens, whether you are part of a police state or part of a bureaucracy, and whether you have access to the media or not.

So, do you think that by the method of research and knowledge we can negate some of those areas of control? Come out on the other side with some greater understanding?

Mal: I don't think there is another side actually. I don't think there is some black hole that you can come out of the end and say, "Great, we've washed the streets clean, now we'll start again."

In the light of that, what is your opinion of the media?

Mal: I think the media is a strengthening of those control bonds that exist already. The media just embellishes them.

Richard: I think that most newspapers are a joke, they are rubbish and it is sad that people believe them. People actually believe what they read in The Sun. You hear people talking, repeating things that they read in the newspapers, believing that they are the absolute truth. I used to read the Morning Star, the communist newspaper, and if you compared what they said about an event, and what The Sun said about it, it was as if you were reading about two different events.

I remember when Tony Benn was standing for the Chesterfield by-election, the Tory gutter press went out to do a smear campaign on him. I can't understand the mentality of these people who write these articles. They are either really clever or really stupid, I can't make up my mind which it is. They write in such a way that is really simple but it is pitting their opinion against public opinion in order to influence people. I find it really sick and sinister as well.

What about TV? Do you agree with the opinion that ours is the best in the world?

Richard: I think it probably is. I've watched TV in quite a lot of other countries and certainly in terms of documentaries Britain seems to be the best.

What about comedy on TV, what sort of things make you laugh?

Richard: Bilko, Russ Abbott. I think one of my all time favourite comedy films is 'The Rebel' with Tony Hancock. It is so well done, you can see people just like the character he plays in the film, wandering about all the time. I'm probably one of them!

In terms of what we do – anybody who can bring out 'Do the Mussolini Headkick' can't be totally serious. That was black humour inspired by a piece of film footage of all those people laying the boot in on old Musso's corpse. I'd draw a comparison with a lot of Bunuel's films – there is something subversive about it, but it is also really funny.

So would you describe your humour as pretty black?

Mal: Yes, I'd love to have seen Tommy Cooper die on TV!

A lot of people wouldn't admit to that. It is a bit taboo to say that there is something funny about someone dying on stage.

Mal: Yes, it is a slightly morbid thing to want to see, but he died happy doing what he wanted. I'd love to see someone die in their moment of glory. Tommy Cooper dying on stage – live on TV – it's like someone dying in battle!

It was a powerful piece of television. I suppose there is a detachment watching that sort of thing on TV – whereas if you went out of your way to go and see it live you would be considered a ghoul.

Mal: It is the sort of detachment that journalists have to have in order to report or film certain things – so as to leave the viewer open to see it. The viewer also has that detachment – because it is on TV the viewer can remain anonymous – rather than actually physically having to go and see it.

Do you think that people flocking to the scene of a disaster is just an extension of that, or is it something more? I couldn't see myself doing that.

Mal: No, I couldn't join in that sort of thing – that goes back to that real 'Sun mentality'.

There is a fine line between journalistic interest and morbid fascination. Most people are happy to watch it on TV and let the cameraman do the dirty work for them.

Mal: Yes, because it gives the viewer a moral detachment from it. It is the same with a lot of the material that we use, the viewer has that anonymity and they can see the things that they want to see.

It is undeniable that people enjoy watching violent images? Is that inevitable? Are people always going to be obsessed with violence?

Mal: People always have been. It has always been the same, it is just the tools and wording have changed over the years. The hypocrisy of it is – that what society rejects are the things that society loves the most. As you say, people do like to watch violent images – so the things we knock the most are the things we want to watch. It is what gets the adrenalin going, it is basic human instinct. It is a fascination, we all love to watch horror films, we all love to hear ghost stories. It makes you more aware of mortality. The actual emotions and issues, and the points raised are the same. The way people are sold violence has never changed. People were sold Hitler in the same way that we are sold nuclear weapons.

Your lists of reading matter and visuals often include a lot of material on Hitler and the Nazis. Why do you think that the Nazis represent a fascination to a lot of people?

Mal: Ironically, although a lot of people wouldn't admit it, much of the fascination stems from the fact that they could perpetrate such atrocities which had such repercussions, but still have this very cosmetic point of style. It is a very cosmetic point about the Nazis, but it is still true, that however much you hate the Nazis, they still had style.

Do you think that the power of Nazi symbolism is what people still find interesting?

Mal: Yes, I think people are very interested in the way that they worked psychologically, which has probably made the Nazis the largest public relations exercise the world has ever seen.

Richard: Oh yeah, they had the best designers working for them of any army I have ever seen. I think it is very powerful imagery, and even today people are saying that the subject is taboo and should be swept under the carpet. There is definitely something to be said for that phrase, "Those who forget the past are condemned to repeat it". I don't think Nazism is something you can forget about and just sweep it away.

sluggin'
fer
jesus

- RELIGION

- CATHOLICISM

- FEAR OF DEATH

- THE OCCULT

You have used religion as a theme fairly extensively, both in your music ('Sluggin' Fer Jesus', 'Red Mecca', 'Three Mantras' etc.) and your visuals. What are your reasons for doing so?

Richard: Our use of religious material is a mischievous thing. I see religion as a totally ridiculous entity, so why not take the piss out of it? That's what is really good about Bunuel's films, I mean he built a whole career around that.

Would you say then that you had no religious beliefs?

Richard: I don't know. No, I don't think I do have any. I tend to believe in a combination of science and mysticism – and that

91

somewhere between the two lies the key. There are so many things that can't be explained purely scientifically at the moment. However, the whole of religion is such a farce, it's just another form of control and repression. It dates back to the inquisition – and before that – when it was used as a tool to create fear in people and keep them in their place, and I think it is still like that.

You always wear a cross around your neck though?

Richard: It's just jewellery as far as I'm concerned. I used to tell people that I wore it to keep the vampires away.

What about your religious beliefs, Mal. Would you describe yourself as a religious person?

Mal: It sounds a bit paradoxical, but I am quite a religious person in that I am aware of it all the time, and I think that is because I was brought up a Catholic. I am not a Catholic now, but I think being brought up as one has really helped me. The whole idea of Catholicism sucks, but nothing has benefited me more than being brought up in that sort of atmosphere, because it gives you some sense of value. It was only after realising that sense of value I could discard it.

So would you say you were an atheist now?

Mal: No I wouldn't because I do believe in something but I'm not sure what it is. I'm a bit of traditional agnostic in that sense – a bit of a liberal. I think the ultimate truth is in yourself. In some respects the religion I believe in is myself, by developing knowledge through experience. First hand knowledge is the main point for me, reaching into yourself, and as a consequence of that, yourself is the only thing that you can ever really find out more about.

Did you both have a religious upbringing?

Richard: Well, I went to a church school, and on Christian religious days we'd have to go to church in the morning and then we'd have the afternoon off. So, in that respect religion was a good thing!

Mal: I was given a very traditional religious upbringing, being brought up by monks and having to go to church every Sunday. It was good in the sense that it really made me realise how much shit there is. Whereas, if you don't have that sort of background there is a tendency not to realise how religious other people are, and more basically what religion actually is.

A lot of the motivation for religion appears to born out of fear – usually the fear of death.

Mal: Both religion and the occult are motivated toward sex and the fear of death. Christianity in a very passive way, and I think the occult is something that negates that.

Richard: It's the fear of damnation or hell-fire or whatever. Like in Islam, where if they don't bury you facing Mecca then you don't go to wherever it is you are supposed to go.

Are you afraid of death. Does it worry you?

Richard: You've caught me on a bad day actually – I'm not feeling too well today! Every now and then I wake up and there's a little nag in the back of my head which says, "I'm going to snuff it one of these days". I suppose everybody gets those, you just push it to the back of your mind and get on with it.

Mal: Yes, we are all subject to an obsession with death, but it doesn't affect my day-to-day living particularly.

When you say obsession with death, do you think it is an obsession that artists are more prone to?

Mal: No, I think we are all much the same. Maybe that little bit of soul searching that artists tend to do elevates it by trying to put death in perspective. Whereas, with other people it is just more subconscious. Everyone is obsessed with sex and death, artists just question it a little bit more, where other people might accept it.

A lot of people, particularly artists and writers, get drawn to religion later in life – Salvador Dali, for example.

Richard: Yes, and Burroughs talking about space travel is just sublimating it into another area. I think as you get older you become more resigned to your fate. It is pretty inescapable! That is unless you are a great believer in reincarnation.

Could you ever see yourself turning to a belief in reincarnation?

Mal: Yes, I suppose so, because I am open to anything. I don't know whether I would go as far as religious conversion though. I think that is why religions are so strong, because a little bit of them exists in everybody. I think it is a bit foolhardy to just dismiss it by saying, "Oh God, that's a load of shit". I don't think you can be too rational, too black and white, about deeply emotive areas. I think the whole notion of religions and mortality is fascinating.

You both also seem to be interested in the occult?

Mal: Yes, I do find it interesting. I think in general there is a resurgence in interest in it – because modern life, and Western society in particular, has eroded people's values to the point where they feel the need to latch onto something or find some sense of being. I don't think that Christian religion has been able to keep up with that need. I find the occult intriguing because of the gradual destruction of the old knowledge of what happened before Christianity – so from a specific and objective point of view I find it interesting to try and find out a little bit more about this old knowledge and the old cultures. I have come to realise how much Christian values have eroded what has gone before.

Richard: My interest in the occult stems from the fact that it is something that you are supposed to shy away from. To a person like myself, if I'm told it is taboo, that just makes it all the more interesting to me and I have got to find out what it is all about. I'm not saying that I'm interested in conjuring up demons, but I don't think you can dismiss the whole thing.

You look at it as tackling one of society's taboos?

Richard: Yes, for example, if you go to the library and look through the index under Aleister Crowley, you will find a long list of titles but you might only find one of them on the shelves, the others are out the back. That makes me wonder why all those other books are not on the shelves?

95

Is your interest totally academic or have you had any direct experiences?

Richard: I think deja vu and coincidences are all experiences of that sort. The whole idea of psychic phenomena really interests me. I recently read a book about psychic discoveries behind the Iron Curtain, it is obviously an area which interests them greatly – although a lot of people are bound to say that they are looking to use it as a weapon against America. I would imagine it is done purely for research, like the people who research into it in England and America, but there are enough people around who will just say, "It's those nasty Russians at it again".

If you start to dig around and look at things from an occult viewpoint, there are a lot of strange coincidences. A friend of a friend did a lot of research into this and he found things leading to addresses in the UN building tying in with UFOs and the men in black. I think there is a hell of a lot to it. I couldn't begin to explain it but there is obviously something strange going on behind the scenes.

It would seem to me that it is easy to draw conclusions from these sorts of coincidences. Do you think the sort of people who do this sort of research are too susceptible to connecting everything they find?

Richard: Yes, in some cases, but I do think it is healthy to always be on the look out. However, it is easy to start reading things into it that aren't there in the first place. You have to watch out for that.

Isn't the occult merely the other side of the coin to religion – just an alternative way of controlling people?

Richard: Like anything else there is bound to be a hierarchy in an occult society, but from what I have read, it is to be used for your own ends rather than someone else telling you what to do, and therefore controlling you.

makes
the
world
round

- MONEY

- THE SIXTIES

- AMERICA

- JAPAN

How do you approach your finances and is financial control very important to you?

Mal: Yes, it is important to us, and we are still aware of what is going on, although not to the extent of doing the bookwork.

So, the Cabaret Voltaire financial set-up is basically two people and an accountant?

Mal: Yes.

Exactly how important is it for someone in your position to remain aware of the finances available to you?

Mal: I think it is very important because it is one of the yardsticks by which you can judge how you are able to develop, and how to continue working. I think there is a real danger of people jumping in and not realising what their true potential is. If you can keep control of the financial side of things – not to the extent of knowing where every penny goes, but at least keeping a clear picture of what's happening – then you are less likely to overstretch yourselves, or take the wrong decisions at the wrong time.

What is you attitude to making money? How do think it would affect you if you made a lot of it?

Mal: It's bound to affect you. There is always the case where you might say that having money would be great because I could put the money to a use – you know, "I am the one who knows how to use it". Howard Hughes, for instance, didn't have a clue how to use the money he made.

Have you any qualms about making money?

Richard: No, not me. If anyone asks me about money and earning it, my answer is always that there is nothing wrong with earning money, it's what you do with it when you have got it that's important. I mean, if you make a lot of money and choose to waste it on indulgence and trash, then I suppose that is fair enough. If I had a lot of money I would put it to some creative use, but I see nothing wrong with making money – I've never said the opposite.

Mal: I think it is a sad state of affairs when people slag you off if you earn a lot of money from what you do – particularly in an artistic way. It's not the money itself, it's the fact that you've made it in that way. Nobody has ever knocked Kraftwerk or Yello for having really rich parents and not having to work at all.

Would you say that your philosophy was basically capitalist – in terms of making the best of what's available to you, and using it to affect people?

Richard: Well, you could say that I was a capitalist, but I see capitalism as a concept based on exploitation, and I don't see that I am exploiting anyone in particular. As far as I can see, we make good music and people pay money to hear it. Fair enough.

Mal: Yes, I agree. I have no qualms about it. I mean, years ago I was anti-capitalist, but I was an idiot. Now I have no qualms about it or about making money. I think if you are in that sort of system you have to utilise it – you have to use those channels and those formulae, meaning that you have to be basically capitalist in your outlook.

So, you believe in the market economy?

Richard: Yes, that's why I would never vote for communism. I suppose you could say that I was a capitalist, but not in the exploitation sense.

It is difficult to ascertain the levels of unemployment under communism, but do you think that in Capitalist countries in the future we will have to accept it as inevitable?

Richard: I think the whole thing relates to the way that society is geared to the work ethic. That is what is drummed into you at school – at least it was when I was brought up. Perhaps now there is mass unemployment people aren't told the same things anymore.

Possibly people need some sort of work ethic to hold on to. For instance, you work pretty hard at what you are doing, but you are in the lucky position of doing the thing you enjoy most for a living.

Richard: Yes, I can see that point of view. Myself it is always a struggle between pleasure and getting on with creative outlets. I don't like getting too lazy. There is only so much time you can spend sitting on your arse drinking beer, or whatever. There is always something nagging me in the back of my head to get on with something useful!

However, the way things are going with the increase in technology and computerisation, the work ethic has become less relevant. Technology is making people redundant, so what are you going to tell people who leave school in five years time?

Have you ever been tempted to spend any of your money on the more typical material things such as cars?

Richard: Well, I have a mortgage and Mal has had one. I have never been motivated to drive, and now I can afford a car I am not that

bothered. I quite often take taxis, which is a bit extravagant, but unlike owning a car you only have to pay for taxis when you use them.

However, I am really fond of 1958 American Chevrolets. I do love those big old cars, and if I did ever own a car it would definitely be one of those. I think they are palaces of kitsch on wheels.

The 50's and 60's produced such wonderful examples of kitsch style because of the relative prosperity. Is it a whole period that fascinates you?

Richard: Yes, I have a soft spot for it even though I wasn't old enough to experience it, but I have read a lot about it in books. It might just have been crap at the time, but on the other hand, a lot of people who did experience the 60's did reckon it was as good as it was made out to be. Some of the things I read in that Warhol book on the 60's ('Popism') just made me green with envy.

What about some of the Beat writers like Kerouac, were influenced by that 'On The Road' mentality?

Richard: Well, I thought 'On The Road' was a bit over romanticised – the whole bit about being a tramp. However, I did get quite a lot of motivation from those books I must admit. I think they changed my attitude toward a lot of things including money, and opened up a lot of avenues. After all, why should you follow others? Why shouldn't you choose your own path, regardless of whether you make money out of it or not?

'On The Road' could only have been written about America. That period in America holds a fascination for a lot of people. To a lot of people America still appears as the ultimate in affluence – what are your impressions of the country when you visit there?

Mal: Well, a lot of our visits are for pure pleasure – we treat it like a holiday, so we tended only to see the good side. However, although we are never there long enough to see the bad side, you still get an impression of it. We have spent quite a bit of time in San Francisco and that is more like a European city. I thought Los Angeles was really the most disgusting place I've ever been to in my life.

Richard: I enjoy America while I'm there – I think it opens your eyes a lot. People might speak the same language as us, but it is still very different.

What is the reaction like when you play out there?

Mal: Really good, For instance, in Los Angeles the people are just totally psychotic – the whole place is on the brink, on a knife edge – and the people just reflect that.

People always say that we are just ten years behind America. Do you think we have got that coming?

Mal: Yes, I mean I can see it happening already. A lot of it is linked to how linked they are to the consumer society – a society with a built in obsolescence, which is what we in Britain are becoming.

Richard: As regards them being ten years ahead I think they are in some ways. Certainly in terms of technology, but I don't think they're ahead culturally speaking. I don't see the same parallel with crime either, because basically there are so many firearms in America – especially with the police being armed. I think violence breeds violence.

You're not exactly renowned as a prolific touring band, so how did you come to play in America in the first place?

Mal: Rough Trade were setting themselves up in America by opening an office on the West Coast. Peter Walmsley, who was the person we worked most closely with at Rough Trade, was the person who went to set it up. He was a friend and a fan, who was continuously working for us while we were at Rough Trade – especially after the incident where we pulled out of the Kleenex and Raincoats tour. He and his girlfriend went to San Francisco, and we went with them almost as a public relations exercise, helping to establish Rough Trade in America. In fact, a lot of the places we have played have been linked to what Peter Walmsley was doing at the time. It was the same with Japan, because Peter was the one who dealt with the licensing.

What were your impressions of Japan?

The group pose infront of Japanese graffiti at the Tsubakihouse.

The ticket that didn't explode.

Richard: One thing I found very interesting about Japan is its split personality – on the one hand they have got all this incredibly high technology, whilst on the other hand you have got people walking around in Kimonos and all the traditional gear. I think I also liked it because everyone was really polite – I don't think I met anyone who was obnoxious the whole time I was there. Generally, I admire the way things are done out there. Particularly the efficiency is something I admire. I can't stand inefficiency. For instance, I always try and be on time – little things like that.

Did you find it a culture shock going to Japan?

Mal: It was a tremendous culture shock, especially the way that their traditional way of life carries on in their psychology. As people, they still retain a very medieval self respect and caste system. It is odd, because they also have this consumer society while still retaining the ideas of self-respect.

They have very much absorbed American culture, the fast food etc. The kids have also absorbed American teen culture like Happy Days and rockabilly – they seem to look toward that trash American culture. Ironically, the Americans have totally shit on them – America still uses Japan as an area to dump nuclear waste and the Japanese just sit there and accept it. I do like them for their self-respect, that is something that has totally fallen here in Britain. However, the bad side of it is that they are very happy to accept their role and bow to whoever.

I think there is going to be a tremendous backlash in Japan. The right wing element is really growing, not in a fascist political way, although that might develop as well, but there is this segment of society that the older generation really resents and this has filtered through to the younger generation. They resent the way that they have been Americanised and lost some of their traditional ways of life. This is more than just a 'back to the land' sort of thing. It is more ethical, where you are getting this type of reversal to the Samurai way in a lot of their thinking.

They seem to have an extraordinarily high set of personal standards and morals.

Richard: Yes, I think that is mainly to do with the difference between Eastern and Western ideals. Their minds seem to work in a totally different way.

Why do you think they like your music?

Richard: I haven't got a clue. I think some of our music may have Eastern leanings.

Could you see yourself living in Japan or America. In fact is there anywhere other than Sheffield that you would consider living?

Richard: Yes, but it probably wouldn't be in England. I would mention Tokyo and San Francisco because they are two of the places out of those I have visited that I have been taken with. I like the idea of living in Tokyo because of the technology that is racing along all the time. I probably couldn't handle living there all year, but maybe for three months or so.

Amsterdam also, I would put that on my list. I like Amsterdam because the people there are really pleasant all the time. There's something abnormal about people who are really pleasant all the time! In terms of living abroad, I quite admire what Bowie has done. He's lived in a lot of different places and obviously if you can afford to do it I think that is a good thing to do. It makes you so much more broad-minded, it opens you eyes to see how different societies and cultures live.

A lot of touring inevitably means a lot of flying. Are you nervous of flying?

Richard: It's not natural is it! It's not the actual sensation that bothers me. Once I've got over the shock that the thing has actually got off the ground, I start to think that there is a lot of distance between me – in this metal cylinder 30,000 feet up – and the ground. I just take some tranquillisers, down loads of booze and put my Stowaway headphones on.

Do you think that you will be under increasing pressure to play more abroad?

Mal: I don't think our touring will increase to the extent that it could do. We are still a very British band – we still look to Britain as

the main litmus test for what we do. We certainly wouldn't want to fall into the trap of touring more instead of developing what we do. I certainly have no interest in flogging the same fucking thing to everyone else.

toward
new
visions

- VISUAL PRESENTATION

- DOUBLEVISION

- VIDEO

- FILM

As a group you have always put a heavy emphasis on the visual side of your presentation. This culminated in you setting up your own video label Doublevision. You obviously considered that there was scope for an independent video label at that time?

Mal: Yes, as we progressed we realised that we were in the position to achieve some of the things that other people had talked about. In particular, the link between the music and the use of visuals, film and video. In our own quiet way we found that we were able to fill a gap in a practical way.

When you set up Doublevision you presumably had a lot of footage accumulated that you had used in live performance over the years. Your first video release, like a lot of the films you use live, contained a great variety of footage including the violent and political as well as fairly anonymous imagery. Was it just a case of throwing in everything but the kitchen sink?

Mal: With the visuals it is very much like that. I don't think we can discard the chance element, the whole idea of the cut-up principle. I think that if we threw that out of either our films or our music, we would probably make everything we have done in the past redundant. I think if we tried to synchronise the visual side with the music, we would be doing nothing more than the early Human League did. With us it is more of a case of chance juxtaposition, but remaining selective about the material we choose to use.

So, it is more of a blanket presentation rather than trying to make a point at any stage?

Richard: That's true to a certain extent. I think it goes back to the Dadaist notion of being mischievous, just playing around juxtaposing different images and sounds and seeing what the end product is.

There would appear to be an amoral attitude in the presentation of a whole range of visual material which leaves people to make of it what they will. Is it important to you not to be making a particular point?

Richard: Yes, because if you do take a moral standpoint it becomes something you are known for, a millstone around your neck that you may get stuck with.

Couldn't you then be criticised for sitting on the fence and hedging your bets?

Richard: Yes, sure.

Also relying heavily on chance elements, aren't you laying yourselves open to the criticism, "Anyone could do that", or are you saying that you have a special instinct for it?

Mal: Definitely an instinct. Only an idiot could believe that it was totally random. It all depends on what you choose to include. That is where you stamp your identity on it. The point is, we choose the

Live at the Tsubakihouse, Japan, March 1982.

Live on Spanish TV, Autumn 1983.

source material, we choose what to cut up, we choose what to juxtapose.

Is your success at this selection process because you have a clearer idea of the images you want to portray, or because your instinct for imagery is better then others?

Mal: I would go for the latter, because we still feel instinctively what will look or sound right – or on the other hand what is not visually right for us.

Richard: I can't really explain a lot of what we do, I don't know why we are doing it half the time. It is only afterwards when I sit down to think about it that it makes any sense. It is a very instinctive thing.

So, it is not actually knowing what you are trying to do, but instinctively feeling it?

Mal: Yes, exactly. I think if we knew exactly what we were trying to do it would be too conceptual, and we are not those sort of people. That is where we differed from Throbbing Gristle, who we were often compared with in the early days. They had a conceptual idea of what they were doing and what they wanted to get across. It's the same with Psychic TV, it is very much a game to them in the sense that they know what they are saying, and if you rumble that you are in. That is all very well, but I don't think we play that sort of game.

From watching some of your videos, it would appear to me that you have been fairly successful in throwing images back at people, especially news footage, that are familiar to them and highlighting those images in a different context.

Mal: I think what we do in a very primitive way is to throw back some of those images. I don't know whether the way we use media footage actually works in terms of people recognising some of the biased and hypocritical aspects of the media – or whether it is just that the pictures look nice and they fit in with the music.

You mean pure flirtation with imagery?

Mal: Yes, exactly. You can talk with hindsight about a lot of these things but I'm sure for a lot of people our use of imagery just looks nice. Maybe that is a lot of the appeal for us as well.

One of Doublevision's releases was the 'TV Wipeout' video which was a sort of disposable video magazine compilation. It contained a fairly wide variety of contributors, from people like The Fall and Test Dept to some more mainstream groups like Bill Nelson and Japan.

Mal: The point was that Virgin Films were quite happy to work with us – they even gave us money in terms of advertising revenue for using some of the clips from the Virgin catalogue. We were then able to camouflage them into the whole set up and make them look as if they were part of the whole nature of the video compilation.

One of the clips was a particularly inane interview with David Bowie. Was its inclusion merely a selling point?

Mal: Yes, it was purely that. There are a lot of people who will buy anything with David Bowie on it. So we said, "Fuck it, why not use that as a pure selling point". Actually the interview is appalling, it's terrible. Our including was almost like a piss take. We were saying, "You really will buy anything with David Bowie on it if you buy this".

I particularly enjoyed the Renaldo and the Loaf piece of film.

Richard: Yes, apparently they are a couple of really normal blokes who live in Portsmouth who happened to meet The Residents when they visited America.

Did you see The Residents when they finally got to play over here?

Richard: Yes, I was a bit disappointed. It was a bit too much like a sixth form drama class with all those tacky drops that kept moving around the stage. Parts of it I quite enjoyed, but it was a bit too much of the concept album scenario. That whole business of 'The Mole Trilogy'. I mean, why bother to try and explain that out?

Doublevision also released the Derek Jarman film 'In the Place of the Sun' on video. How did that come about?

119

Richard Kirk contemplates the keyboard.

The group with a 'psychedelic' back projection.

Richard: Derek Jarman has his own film company called Dark Pictures which he set up in conjunction with 2 or 3 other people. I think they got in touch with us with regard to releasing the video.

It seems to me that Derek Jarman as an independent film-maker has the balance about right between the avant garde and the realistic.

Richard: Yes, I watched Jubilee again recently, and I think it watches a lot better now than it did when it came out. I don't know whether my attitude has changed or whether I've become a bit more educated about certain things, but it seemed to make a lot more sense now.

In terms of film makers Bunuel is someone who seems to interest you particularly. Have you read his autobiography, 'My Last Breath'?

Richard: Yes, I have. I was impressed with the way that he described how they made 'Un Chien Andalou' – they just got their finger out and went and did it. It is reading that sort of thing that makes me think that it is about time that we got up and did something like that. Also, he describes how, when they were making 'Un Chien Andalou', they put in a lot of pieces that had no meaning, reason or logic. That has always appealed to me.

Generally up to now you have always stressed that you put your ideas across in a very unstructured way. Can you envisage that method of working ever changing?

Mal: Yes, with video I can envisage us taking a more structured approach, because it is a more controlled medium. I think with the use of editing techniques you can emphasise certain things and still keep it stimulating, whilst still retaining some chance elements. When we finished editing the Doublevision Cabaret Voltaire video we decided that it was the last time we would do that sort of grainy video. The texture of the video was nice, it worked well, but we would never want to do that again.

However, I can't envisage us taking a more structured approach in terms of live performance. Live performance has got to be spontaneous – it has got to have that chance element. If you take that element out, you take out all the fun for us.

So, if you were to make a film, for instance, would you take a more structured approach?

Richard: It is a case of making some kind of structure and fitting that in context. I think that is what we would want to do with a film, actually take it one step further and put it to some use, make it do something.

Could you imagine producing something that was scripted?

Richard: I don't know whether we would stretch to a narrative running through it or whether it would be scripted. Whether a narrative would make any point or a script any sense is another matter. In some respects a script and dialogue would force us to be more structured. It would be a case of learning where we would need to take a more calculated approach as we went along. What we hope to do with the visuals would be similar to what we have done with the recent music, and that is to produce a more disciplined order of things, but within that use the cut-up technique. So, the cut-up principle would be used more to some effect, and less as an end in itself.

However, you will be concentrating mostly on the music for the moment?

Richard: Obviously, as it provides our main source of income. If we didn't make records we couldn't do the visuals because we couldn't afford the resources.

Are there any other areas in which you are interested in getting involved? For instance, in an old interview I remember reading once that you were interested in opening a club.

Richard: The more you go on, the more you realise the impracticalities of a thing like that. You begin to realise why other people haven't done it.

Factory's Hacienda club, for instance, very soon turned into just another rock venue.

Richard: That is how it ended up – all the prices went up. You can't really do it, even if you take over an established club one night a week. The only thing that comes close to what I would want to do are the Jamaican Blues Clubs where the police won't touch them. Just somewhere to go.

Is there not a potential for some sort of video club where videos could be shown on a more ambient level, rather than having to sit and watch them?

Richard: Well, we did a video performance at the Hacienda that nobody came to, and it went along its own little way. The videos got shown and people wandered around, some of them watched some of them didn't. There was only a couple of hundred people there, which was little bit daunting in a place as big as the Hacienda. I think we learned how not to do it. The next time we do something like that it will be better.

One thing that has struck me as surprising about your live presentations is that you have nearly always stuck solidly to playing and performing at established rock venues.

Mal: The reason why we play established rock venues is because we tread a thin line between being the arty band and the ordinary band.

Richard: It was a conscious decision to play those places because we hated the performance art side of it. Doing the sort of music we did, it would have been really obvious to do gigs in performance art places. We felt that to achieve anything we had to take it to rock places. I think it goes back to the provocation, putting on things like we did infront of people who were used to rock 'n' roll. That was where the appeal lay. Perhaps we should do the reverse now!

You have occasionally played less rock-orientated sets. You did a sort of video presentation in Belgium.

Richard: The Belgian show was more fun than the video evening at the Hacienda. I was really into the idea of intimidating the Belgians, because it was advertised that we were supposed to be playing – someone fucked us over somewhere there. It was great, we appeared in total darkness and people complained that we weren't even on stage! Blaine, who used to be in Tuxedo Moon, would go on stage before the shows and start winding the audience up and insulting them. He would make up all these ridiculous names for

THE FINAL ACADEMY

READINGS ★ MUSIC ★ PERFORMANCE ★ FILM ★ VIDEO ★ EXHIBITION

William Burroughs is the only American novelist working today who may conceivably be possessed of genius — Norman Mailer

For the first time ever WILLIAM BURROUGHS reads in London.

The Final Academy is a Programme of Events celebrating William Burroughs

A rare opportunity to see William Burroughs with his lifetime collaborator BRION GYSIN, and JOHN GIORNO, one of the greatest New York live poets, reading in England.

We have assembled a programme of events that will provide the British public with a unique opportunity to experience this legendary figure, a man who has not only revolutionised literature but is one of the mainstays of pop culture.

THE FINAL ACADEMY brings together a diverse range of talents spanning three generations throughout which William Burroughs has been a hero figure whose influence has been crucial, from the beat generation to the present day. THE FINAL ACADEMY has brought together some of the most original and exciting contemporary artists.

THE FINAL ACADEMY is not a homage but a development towards the future:

PSYCHIC TV ● CABARET VOLTAIRE ● 23 SKIDOO ● IAN HINCHLIFFE ● LAST FEW DAYS ● Z'EV ● JEFF NUTTALL ● PAUL BURWELL/ANNE BEAN ● ROGER ELY/RUTH ADAMS ● TERRY WILSON ● JOHN GIORNO ● BRION GYSIN ● WILLIAM BURROUGHS

The continuing legacy of William Burroughs and Brion Gysin

David Dawson
Roger Ely
Genesis P-Orridge

THE FINAL ACADEMY

bands. At one point there were three different groups on stage just churning out some kind of noise!

The Belgian shows were directly after you played the third night of The Final Academy. The whole event was an attempt to mix readings by Burroughs and Gysin with some of the contemporary groups who have been influenced by them. What was your opinion on the success of that?

Mal: I was quite disappointed with it. I found it very establishment, very arty, very strict. Very gallery-ish.

Richard: I spoke to Gen quite a few times about a year before it was organised and I don't think it was his intention to make it cosy and cliquey. I don't think he viewed it like that at all. I think it was successful insomuch as it brought a lot of people together with similar aims and a similar outlook on things.

The whole thing did seem to be very strict. People being forced into seats and no bar etc.!

Richard: Just because the Final Academy was a literary thing, why shouldn't there be a bar? Why shouldn't people be able to wander round. The idea of seated venues is horrible.

Mal: It didn't appeal to the people it was meant to. It was too strait-laced. What was on show was supposed to be contemporary poetry, music and literature but it seemed to have no spirit or spontaneity. I think the organisation of the event was so difficult that it had to be done like that, but half the time I felt like I was watching an auction.

Richard: The whole thing failed in the same way as the Kodo drummers did when I went to see them recently. It was like seeing them in a church, you couldn't speak in case someone turned round and told you to shut up. I didn't like that whole atmosphere.

Do you think the Final Academy was over ambitious? Do you think that an event like that could ever work?

Mal: I think it could, but not in England, and certainly not at the Brixton Ritzy! In retrospect it seemed very clinical, it didn't seem to have an awful lot of life of its own. However, we were only there on one night. I thought Burroughs was good though.

Richard: I thought he was hilarious. He's a great stand up comic that bloke.

Is it true you met him in Belgium once?

Richard: Yes, it was a few years ago now. It was more a case of just sitting around around a table drinking champagne and listening to him. There was some French geek asking him what he thought of Suicide. Burroughs started talking on about people killing themselves – obviously he had never heard of the group. I gave Burroughs a Cabaret Voltaire badge.

That was in 1979, when you were on the bill with Joy Division amongst others at Le Plank.

Richard: Yes, and in some respects that whole thing was a lot more successful than the Final Academy. It was held in this sort of arts centre, which had a bar for one thing! There were a whole load of things going on. They had a bloke playing improvised saxophone at one end of the building and Burroughs was on a different floor doing his readings. There were TV monitors everywhere so you could see what was going on. They were showing all Burroughs' films in another room.

Somehow you could never imagine that sort of event happening in Britain.

Richard: We can't get our shit together here. I think in Europe there is so much more money available for that sort of thing. For instance, that whole Le Plank event was sponsored by the government. The same is true in America where there seems to be the facilities to get things done. Certainly with regard to something like big budget films, the money always seems to be there somewhere. For instance, John Carpenter made Dark Star while he was still at college. You certainly couldn't do that here. The money must be available in England – it is just that the Arts Council grants go to the biggest wankers imaginable.

I think a lot of it boils down to the fact that we seem to be really embarrassed by the arts in this country.

By 1984 the 'music industry' had fully embraced Cabaret Voltaire, despite their claim of being 'non musicians'.

Richard: Yes, they always seem to be discredited. At school there were kids who were shit hot artists, but they never seemed to be encouraged. People in this country don't consider the arts to be a genuine way to earn your living, unlike a plumber or a decorator. Art tends to only be thought of as OK as a hobby.

Returning to the visual side of your performance, you nearly always play infront of a video backdrop. However, at one of your shows in Sheffield 1983 you played in front of a bank of televisions. Do you think that was the most successful visual presentation you have attempted?

Richard: Well, it would have been if most of them had worked! I was quite impressed with the way it looked. It was a one-off thing though.

Mal: I thought it was pretty good, the whole thing worked really well on that one night – it might not work on another night.

Do you consider yourselves as entertainers when you play live, or are the films the entertainment?

Richard: I don't know, it's a bit of a grey area to me.

Mal: I don't know really – it is almost like the whole meaning of the word entertainment has changed since we started. I don't see ourselves as strictly entertainers – if people find it entertaining then that's OK. People dance more at some of the gigs. I don't know what we are live, we just perform and enjoy what we are doing.

Would you think of expanding into more sophisticated live shows?

Richard: No, in terms of the music, that was one of the bad things about the tour we did in 1983 as far as I was concerned. We kind of rushed into it and went for the easy option of putting things down on tape. That was fair enough, but I don't think I would want to do that again. I'd rather make it a lot more improvised, because I get a lot more out of it when it is like that. However, playing to backing tapes was an interesting exercise in discipline – actually having to restrict yourself to a certain format.

In terms of the visuals, that is another thing we are re-thinking. The whole thing with the films and slides is getting a bit boring. People expect us to have films, so maybe it is about time to change them. At one stage we did go through a phase when we didn't always use films, it all depended on the suitability of the venue. Some days we just didn't bother with it. It would be quite nice to do a few shows again without back projections. I mean if you go to any gig in Sheffield these days, the chances are you're going to see a back projection. I'm not saying we invented it or anything.

Mal: I also think that we have got to be careful in the way we use the visuals – we don't want to turn into a Pink Floyd! It works on a crude level but we've got to avoid over- sophistication and avoid creating a white elephant.

I suppose it must be difficult in some respects because you never get to see the full effect of it at the time.

Richard: I quite often just turn round and watch the films. I can remember particularly enjoying them when we played in Berlin once. Mind you part of that was due to other reasons!

Do you always have a drink or something before you play live?

Richard: No, I have done loads of gigs straight, but I don't know which is best. It's like when we're mixing an album – part of it is done straight and part of it isn't. It is an interesting way of working. For instance, we might start setting up mixing completely stone cold sober, and then when you get down to the actual mix it is like voodoo time – you've got to get some magic going.

The only area of the visual side to your work we haven't touched upon is the promotional video. I thought the video to 'Just Fascination', and in some respects the one to 'Crackdown', were a dilution of your ideas – a compromise.

Mal: I think it was a psychological thing. It's a horrible thing being signed to a major label when it affects you psychologically. I think because it was our first video for Virgin, we thought we would play the game, and we played it too safe and watered it down. It was mostly our fault and not Pete Care's. I think in his own way Pete made a very good, subtle video and the more I see it the more I see the subtleties. It was Pete's video really and we gave him full rein,

The release of the Crackdown LP on Some Bizarre/Virgin was followed by considerable interest from the music press.

and therefore it was his interpretation. Whereas with 'Crackdown' it was more of a conscious effort between us and Pete.

Richard: I think the 'Just Fascination' video was made purely with the intention of getting it shown on TV.

So you think that if you had done something more like the Doublevision cassette it wouldn't have got shown on TV?

Richard: It would have been pretty pointless because we had already done that. We did get part of the Doublevision cassette shown on TV, I don't know how mind you!

Out of those two promotional videos that we did, 'Just Fascination' looked very slick and professional, but of the two everyone prefers 'Crackdown'. It was much more interesting since it was done as an extra and the pressure was off.

In some ways, slickness doesn't seem to fit in with your image.

Richard: I think with the 'Just Fascination' video, not very much happens in it. I'm not knocking it, certainly when you compare it against some of the crap that passes itself off as promos. It is far better than most of those which I have seen – but it was pretty minimal.

Are there any promotional videos you have seen that have impressed you?

Mal: I think most of them are crap. I can't think of any particular one. I don't think anyone has broken the format.

Do you think that it is inevitable that most promos are crap?

Richard: Yes. I think it is especially a shame as there is so much bloody money available to do them. Obviously the director of the video, unless it is someone particularly famous, has got to please the record company who is paying him or he is not going to get any more work. After all, a promo that can't get shown on TV is not really worth much to a record company however good it is.

It still remains that you are one of the most under-televised groups considering the position you have reached.

Richard: We are hoping that is going to change. We are not going to do any live dates for the moment, so we are trying to get more TV so we can get across more in that way.

Anything you would like to say before the tape runs out?

Richard: Well, something that I've thought a lot about is the concept of amassing money. I'm really into the idea – and I'm waiting my turn to play the ultimate Dadaist joke. It could take any form – it could be in a film. But you have got to have a lot of money to do anything that would have a lot of repercussions – apart from an act of terrorism like shooting the president or something!

part
two

1984
to
1988

PART TWO – 1984-1988

Cabaret Voltaire's marriage to Some Bizarre started with the glittering wedding of 'The Crackdown', through the growing pains of 'Microphonies' and 'Drinking Gasoline', and ended in divorce proceedings with the low point of 'The Covenant, The Sword And The Arm Of The Lord'. The marriage, like any other, was full of the usual marital ups and downs, mishaps, near misses and bad timing. One of the ups was a widened audience through the more up front positive approach displayed by a Some Bizarre and Virgin promotion. The records began to be played to a limited degree on the radio, and to a greater degree in the clubs, and the group even made occasional TV appearances. The single of 'Just Fascination' charted at number 74 only to disappear the week after. It would not have been unfair to assume that with a mixture of the photogenic Mallinder and the funk workouts of Kirk, the group were poised for greater things.

This assumption was enhanced by a series of critically acclaimed singles that culminated in 'Sensoria', a melding of 'Do right' and 'Sensoria' off the 'Microphonies' album. With the help of M's Robin Scott they produced a scorching dance track from the ashes of two mediocre LP tracks. Added to this, Pete Care's video for the track reached new heights in their visual cut-up technique infusing a discipline and subtlety into the clipped imagery. The video went on to win a Los Angeles Times video award and Pete Care went on to produce videos for Depeche Mode, Killing Joke and Robbie Neville amongst others.

This standard was both developed and disbanded in the group's video collection entitled 'Gasoline In Your Eye'. The collection comprised of videos for some of their singles together with footage that was at one stage to be the film 'Earthshaker'. The final product was both enlightening and infuriating. It did prove that there was life still in the cut-up method of the group, but the persistent randomness and incessant footage from tours (holidays) abroad reduced the imagery at times to a dull repetitive thud. This having been said, when placed alongside the video output of most groups it proved that Kirk's editing could still carve out a video-scape way beyond most of his contemporaries.

The downs were a withdrawal back into a recording shell that most of the time saw Kirk producing relentless backing tapes in seclusion at Western Works, and Mallinder on visits from London adding a vocal which at times seemed half-baked and devoid of incision. The results of this were some rambling LP tracks that without the visual accompaniment lacked direction. 'Drinking Gasoline' following on so closely from 'Microphonies' was doomed to obscurity.

In the early days their reliance on Western Works had given them the freedom to work at their own pace – now it appeared as if it were to become a limiting factor. The new dance-based material was crying out for refinement that Western Works alone could not provide. When the group did stray into a fully commercial studio even just for the purposes of re-mixing, the difference in terms of results could be devastating, as was the case with 'Sensoria'. When Western Works did finally close, after numerous break-ins, the group moved the studio to another location, leaving behind the memories of many recording sessions – not to mention drinking sessions!

The group also continued to be dogged by mishaps. For instance, the labels for 'Drinking Gasoline' (a double 12") were stuck on the wrong records. It was the type of error they might have hoped to have left behind in the ever chaotic corridors of Rough Trade.

By 1986 one would have been forgiven for assuming that the Cabaret Voltaire bandwagon was grinding to a halt. The group had toured America in 1985 with some success, and in early 1986 played some dates in England that had some elements of going through the motions. In terms of records, they released one single on their own label Doublevision which placed them back in the independent charts in exactly the same place that they had been several years before. The group had quipped on occasions, "We only ever had one idea, and we don't remember what that was". The statement was sounding less like an off the cuff one-liner and more like a sad reality. Doublevision, initially intended to be primarily a video label was dormant apart from the occasional record release – Paul Smith its main administrator concentrating on his own label Blast First. The group also seemed to have abandoned any aspirations they may have had in the area of film.

So, what had gone wrong? The musical 'industrial' revolution was well and truly over. TG was a mere memory, PTV now a hotchpotch of the mystical and magickal under the direction of their guru Genesis P-Orridge, who had managed to mutate from a mischievous philosopher into a bloated dictator of 'psychic people' everywhere. Most of the other spin-offs from that era, when musical barriers had been redefined much as painting had been in the '20s and writing in the '50s, appeared in the late '80s as nothing more than post beat generation groupies, wearing Burroughs on their sleeve and the Velvet Underground on their turntables. Of those groups who had carried on waving the 'alternative' banner, most of their doodlings in sound experimentation now seemed quaintly self-indulgent and at times sadly outdated in a late '80s music scene that craved commerciality.

Cabaret Voltaire, amongst others, had wisely turned more and more toward funk-based dance music as a way of disseminating their sounds. With samplers and sequencers, the dance-floor not only seemed a better form of attack, but was also strangely more closely allied to their original intention than carrying the banner of alternative music through the independent charts to an ever decreasing elite of aficionados of 'industrial' music. The crashing sledgehammer beat and computerised bass lines now being used by a lot of the dance music of the '80s seemed to provide a good base for them on which to build sounds. The crossover was nearly complete

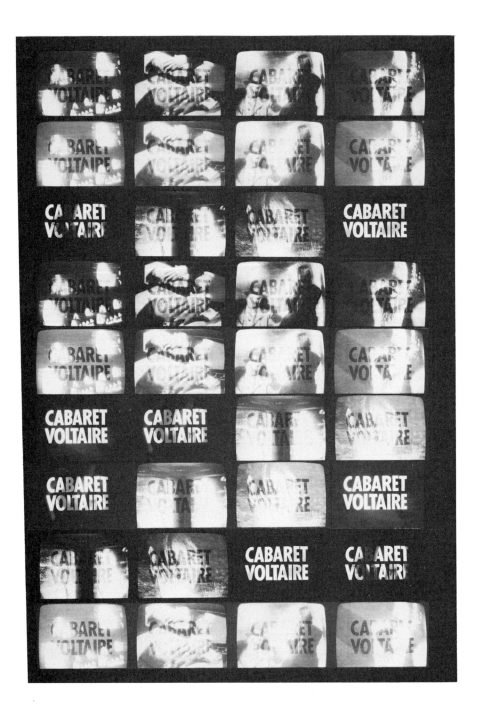

for those who had chosen to take the same path – both New Order and The Fall had both been shadowing the same steps toward the more radical mainstream – with the only difference being that these groups had achieved chart success by 1987. The trouble was that Cabaret Voltaire now found themselves wading in the same water as the likes of Depeche Mode, almost appearing like leather clad elder brothers to the boys from Basildon. The question remained, if they fell in the water in such company, could they swim?

The truth was, at that time they didn't appear to want to find out. The problem of how to reach a chart audience remained, and the answer to the problem seemed to lie with the fact that they were stuck producing sound-scapes rather than songs, melodies or hook lines. They were still piecing together a jigsaw of sounds, that at best was invigorating dance music, but was at worst was a meandering funk output devoid of that necessary hook line. It was no coincidence that their most most successful tracks were always those that kept closest to a song structure. Ironically, 'Nag, Nag, Nag', the single that put them on the map – seemed to do just that. However, the duo were understandably reluctant to throw away the cut-up/random ethic that had carried them through a decade of dabbling and gained them their reputation in the first place.

So, they continued to insist that they were not musicians, a claim that with each LP was beginning to sound more and more of an arrogant posture than a reality. Quite evidently when they started they could not have been termed musicians and Cabaret Voltaire was far from most people's idea of a music group. However, with the advancing years of working and gaining experience within the music business, it was now really impossible to view them in any other light than just another music group. "We're not in the business of crafting pop singles", was a quote. But it became increasingly evident that perhaps underneath it all that is what they should have been trying to do, without worrying whether it compromised any great principle. Some would even go as far as to say that they even deserved to be finding themselves a place in the charts. It was now a fact that many of the successful funk and dance records that were racing past them and into the charts were using a 'found' vocal track over a hard rhythm, a technique they had nurtured and as near as damn it invented some ten years earlier. It was soon to become an audio technique that would become fully absorbed into the media, being used in TV advertising and radio jingles, but very few would appreciate where its origins lay.

By late 1986 fortunes could have been on the turn again. Although Virgin through Some Bizarre had been prepared to extend their recording agreement, EMI were prepared to invest more in a group whose world-wide sales were steady – and who always attracted a good size audience when they played live. Adrian Sherwood was brought in to produce the new material, and working again under the constraints and guidance of a producer it seemed more likely that the group's music would develop better than when they were left to their own devices. Now fully established on a major label it was obvious that the group were going to have to "deliver the goods" in terms of a hit single or increased album sales – EMI's confidence was such that they bought up the Cabaret Voltaire name. At the same time, a collection of the early material now became available through Rough Trade on Compact Disc, a strange irony as some of the material had been recorded on such basic equipment. Also, a collection of their mid period 12" funk workouts was released on Les Disques Du Crepescule helping to highlight how well in advance of trends they had once been.

The LP 'Code' went some of the way to justifying EMI's confidence by showing an improvement in sales, due mainly to an American release – which was aided by sporadic dates Stateside. As with many groups, their fortunes were fairing far better in America and Europe where their reputation was gaining considerably – but at home it appeared just like another example of Britain turning its back on its exports. The singles 'Don't Argue' and 'Here to Go' failed to make any greater indent on the charts than earlier singles had done, and the lavish Las Vegas shot 'Don't Argue' video failed to get much of a showing in Britain, although it continued in the innovative mould of 'Sensoria'.

What many involved with the group regarded as a watershed came at the end of 1987. Although 'Code' had been greeted by poor critical acclaim in Britain, world-wide sales were encouraging, but internal arguments became unresolved about the promotion of the material and about what image the group should be presenting. The disagreements centred around the doing of promotional work and how to approach playing live – in essence whether to respond to the pressure and to present a more up front image in line with their promotion to EMI's ranks. Richard's inherent distrust of becoming too entangled within the shallow niceties of the 'pop music' business – always one of the group's strengths in the past – coupled with his dislike of the amount of flying that would be involved with a busy promotion schedule, was now directly at odds with Mal's idea of how they should be promoting themselves. This situation was not helped by financial problems which were now to beset the group as the taxman started to knock on their door.

What was certain was that by early 1988 the two members' individual positions had become so entrenched that for a time a reconciliation seemed unlikely. The move to EMI, although appearing a step upwards, had in fact temporarily forced a wedge between the two, the question being whether to respond and conform to the full rigours of the 'pop' business. Could it be that the years of sitting on the fence – of waiting for people to come to them – were to backfire on them? Perhaps their inability to take a direction and relying purely on instinct had fallen prey to big business pressure? Or, maybe the individual ambitions of the two were to simply part company. On Some Bizarre/Virgin they had inhabited a comfortable space they had carved out for themselves of semi- experimentalist/semi popstars, on EMI in the pop climate of the late '80s that space was closing up, and the decision of what side of the fence to sit on had to be made. For a few months during 1988 they seemed to be sitting on different sides of that fence.

By mid '88 tensions relaxed and it appeared that the group were merely down and not out. They had decided not to officially split up, typically as ever keeping their options open. In the meantime both had involved themselves in solo recording – Mal in colloboration with Dave Ball and Richard Gordon under the name Love Street, and Richard under the name Wicky Wacky. However, the two were already making moves towards a reconciliation and it again seemed likely that there would be further material from Cabaret Voltaire. The realisation that it was probably too late to start launching solo careers, together with the financial benefits of remaining a group, began to override any personal differences that had arisen between the two.

Whether this latest incarnation of the group will see them ready to come back fit for a final assault on the pop charts, or whether they will continue to remain the Northern jovial pranksters who skirted and flirted with the fringes of popular music, innovated and annoyed – but who were ultimately amongst those influential groups that got away – remains to be seen.

It has been a long time since they sat around the pubs of Sheffield, the sound of a tape loop emanating from the tape recorder on the table, re-enacting dadaesque jokes. Fifteen years on, much of the initial mystique may have gone, some of surreal veneer been a bit tarnished. However, Cabaret Voltaire have managed to carve themselves a unique place both inside and outside the pop music scheme of things – the once notorious sound manipulators turned dancefloor 'beat'sters. They have probably tampered sufficiently by fraying the edges of popular music to ensure their position within its hallways of notoriety if not its hallway of fame. And perhaps more importantly, somewhere along the street 'The Cabs' are still for hire, a little battered but meters running, and sometime yet the last resounding laugh might just be with them.

richard
kirk

RICHARD H. KIRK

Artistically, paranoia is the condition that Richard Kirk inhabits most effectively. The paranoic state is not only one of suspicion, but of confusion and deception. Kirk's clipped imagery, whether in the form of a video, or as a backdrop to their live performance, can appear at first glance as a video jigsaw. On closer inspection of the early videos there seeps through a paranoic subconscious. Politics is bevelled from footage of oppression, sex from the neon pornographia of the Reeperbahn, and religion from self-doubt and fear. These clips of 'found television' are interspersed with footage of the group and the various locations that they have visited. Somehow Kirk manages to instill in the viewer a feeling of claustrophobia. Of not only being stuck within the frame of the body, but also the mind. In some early correspondence he wrote that a Cabaret Voltaire concert is like a bad trip. The imagery at times has hallucinatory tendencies, giving the viewer glimpses of some horror or atrocity that is never quite on screen.

Kirk comments in the RE Search Industrial Culture handbook that his obsessions are Kitsch, pornography and firearms. By coincidence or contrivance, the grand-master paranoic Burroughs also quotes pornography and firearms as objects of obsession in his fiction – and in real life has become an avid collector of firearms. Burroughs' paranoia in his early writing was created from a fabric of heroin addiction coupled with an inbuilt sense of the upturning of words to create quasi-futuristic landscapes where the future could leak out. The framework and manifestations of control; political, religious and social, created a setting for his often humorous heros to drift in and out of. Kirk has stated in the past that his favourite book was probably 'Naked Lunch'. It is certain that this book provides us with the most harrowing and humorous vision of Burroughs' world. Although it is more probable that 'The Job' and 'The Electronic

Revolution' in terms of ideas had the most influence on Cabaret Voltaire amongst others in the '70s, particularly in the references to the power behind tape recorders. It almost goes without saying that Burroughs' belief that cutting up and rearranging things reveals the true nature of them was, and still is, central to the group's thinking.

It was inevitable that Cabaret Voltaire would forge a strong association and friendship with the other main practitioners of musical extrapolations of Burroughs' work, Throbbing Gristle. TG always represented a harsher interpretation of a similar idea compared with Cabaret Voltaire's more tempered and humorous approach. TG were the clinical mass murderers of sound, opening up suppurating sores for the listener and viewer in order to achieve an "entertainment through pain". Kirk was probably the most allied to TG, and a solo tape of his recordings, 'Disposable Half-Truths' appeared on TG's label Industrial records. Accompanied by a xeroxed hand-out, the tape saw Kirk immerse himself into his obsessions producing material that was more dense and inaccessible than that of Cabaret Voltaire. The hand-out was typical of that which had accompanied some of the group's early work, showing a direct nod in the direction of group's other main starting influence of Dadaism.

The German groups of the early seventies were a major influence on Cabaret Voltaire, and Kirk in particular. Probably the most influential of these on Kirk and a host of others including John Lydon, Pete Shelley and Mark E. Smith, who cited them as an influence, were Can. The group existed in various line-ups from the late '60s. However, it is generally accepted that their finest work was produced by the nucleus of Holger Czukay, Irmin Schmidt, Jaki Lieberzeit and Michael Karoli together with Japanese vocalist Damo Suzuki. Karoli's scratchy rhythm guitar and eastern European lead guitar style are easily recognisable in some of Kirk's early playing. Mallinder's consistent two note basslines also bore a similarity to that of Czukay's, although this may have been born more out of a lack of ability on the instrument on Mallinder's part rather than the influence of Czukay, who approached his minimal bass playing from a more musical standpoint. Irmin Schmidt's uncanny ability to play a set of keyboards without ever making the sounds of traditional instruments had the largest influence on Chris Watson.

Both Schmidt and Czukay were ex-students of Stockhausen who took their mentor's parameters of music and infused it into a rock music format, taking elements from ethnic music and reggae shuffle through to the sound of radio interference. At their best they produced shimmering rhythmical soundtracks pinned down to vinyl by Lieberzeit's efficient and repetitious back beat.

The strong element of repetition used by Can, and many of the other German groups of that time like Kraftwerk and Neu, were to have a strong influence on Kirk and the other two members of Cabaret Voltaire. Repetition was, and still is, an element that crops up everywhere in the music of Cabaret Voltaire. There were times when it was used in an avant garde way for the sake of extremeness, and other times when it was used to mirror ethnic or tribal music. Cabaret Voltaire at times were able to capture these two strains just as Can had a few years earlier. However, they managed to instil it with a much harder, what some people termed 'industrial', edge. Coming from the North of England and having some ideas on style and presentation, they managed to avoid the 'hippyish' imagery that some of Can's material conjured up.

Of the two members that now comprise Cabaret Voltaire, Richard represents the 'no compromise' personality within the group. This manifests itself in a number of areas. He is far less open to criticism of the group's work. He also staunchly refuses to be lured to London for its convenience as the centre of the music business in England. He is also more stoically uninterested or unimpressed with the peripheries of the music business. He once described his influences as anything which is unacceptable. However, his primary influence now would appear to be hard dance music. The man who was once happy to listen to a tapeloop of a sledge hammer at a deafening volume that would have sent most scampering for the cotton wool, is now more interested in crafting dancefloor rhythms from an ever increasing array of electrical gadgetry. Visually, although he quotes Bunuel and Fellini as influences, there appears little in common with either film maker in the visual side of Cabaret Voltaire. Their videos seem to have much more in common with the attractive crudity of Warhol's films, where scenes are not so much crafted as thrown together with an abandon and disregard to the art of film-making.

There always appeared to be an artistic ethic within Cabaret Voltaire, they managed to appear art conscious without necessarily becoming 'arty'. Kirk commented on Spanish TV in 1983 that he considered that Cabaret Voltaire started out by being dadaists then became surrealists and were now producing pop art. Ironically, if you were to take the last of these literally it is pop art, or the fusion of art and pop that remains the most difficult ambition to achieve in a culture that is mostly involved in the immediate and disposable.

Finally as a personality Richard Kirk remains shy and retiring, with a dry sense of humour. He once commented on having to buy a music paper which featured the group on the front cover that, "I must be the only person who buys his Sounds wrapped in a copy of Playboy." Recently a passion for good nights out has turned more to good nights in. He continues to live in Sheffield with his girlfriend Lyn who has been involved with the group since the early days.

How has your attitude towards making music and the music business changed over the last few years?

Richard: A lot more cynical more than anything else, but it is still basically the same. I think you just get more cynical as the time goes on.

What has been the difference between Virgin and EMI, have you found it more constricting being on a larger label?

Richard: No, we have complete freedom. The only time we've run into a problem is when we made a video – but in terms of the music, the choice of producers, the choice of studio, we've had no interference at all. I mean I'm not saying that it might not change in the future.

What about your attitudes towards playing live?

Richard: I mean, it has been talked about, it has become a bit of a bone of contention. It's something that we've held back on because of not wanting to just present the same thing. If you upgrade the music it makes sense to upgrade the way it is played live. It's a difficult decision – we don't want to get in loads of musicians and that, but at the same time the idea of performing with two people doesn't seem right somehow.

So, if you were to use other musicians, presumably you wouldn't be putting such a heavy emphasis on backing tapes?

Richard: Well, basically backing tapes are just a way of storing information – and that can be upgraded by doing it with computers. I think maybe using live percussion again would be quite a good thing. So even if we are using backing tapes it makes it more live. The last time we played live in 1986, a lot of what we actually did was live, half of it was on backing tapes and half of it was using sequencers and live drums – it seemed to work quite well. The other problem is the material we have recorded for EMI is a lot more ordered, so we're faced with the problem of having to present that live or making it much looser as it has been in the past. Basically it is the difficulty of not trying to repeat ourselves.

Would I be right in saying that you are less keen on the live work than Mal is?

Richard: Mmmm. (pause)

What about the promotional aspects of the work?

Richard: I've never particularly seen that as my role anyway. I've never been a great one for doing lots of interviews and stuff like that. A lot of that is down to the fact that a lot of the people who we seemed to get interviewed by harp on about Rough Trade and why we left and things like that. The questions don't seem to be as interesting. It doesn't stimulate me as much as it used to, but I mean, a lot of the interviews have been confined more specifically to the 'pop press'.

Is it that the questions have become less interesting or have you become more cynical about the kinds of questions you get asked?

Richard: I mean obviously, that's there. A lot of it seems to be people asking why we moved to EMI. I thought that would have been particularly obvious!

For the money?

Richard: Well, it's a bigger machinery. Also the other thing is America – we never had an American release with Virgin. That's changed and it has worked quite well in terms of getting records pushed and everything.

A lot of the music in the charts at the moment uses heavy rhythm tracks with bits of found voices, things that you have traditionally been associated with. Basically, they are getting the records in the charts and you as yet have not. Are they presenting it in a different way that makes it more commercial?

Richard: I don't know, as you say, it amazes me. We have had a really bad response from the people who take the records into Radio One. I think it's just to do with the name and the history, it almost seems to work against us.

Will you carry on using the clips of found voices in the future in the light of that?

Richard: I think we've tended to use that less and less. On the last record, I think that side of it is played down. When it's there, it's really pushed to the front like on 'Don't Argue'. But that sort of use of it we decided not to do too much of. We mainly used tapes of things – not spoken pieces – but just for sounds.

The last time we spoke you were talking of the music developing in a schizophrenic way – with the dance music but also some atmospheric stuff as well.

Richard: I can't really see EMI going for 20 minute a side ambient records – but where that would work well is with film soundtracks like the one we did for 'Salvation'.

Wasn't one of Doublevision's initial intentions to provide a release for that sort of material, but you haven't used it much of late. Is the label dead or just dormant?

Richard: It's dormant – it's not dead by any means. A lot of the actual day to day work has been delegated to Factory's video label, Icon. They handle the distribution, the manufacturing and everything.

Have there been any recent Doublevision releases?

Richard: No. Not to my knowledge anyway! (laughs)

Are there going to be any in the near future?

Richard: There was a compilation album that was being put together but it ground to a halt. I think that a lot of it has to do with the fact that everybody has been too involved doing other things. Paul Smith who is the main driving force behind Doublevision in terms of getting things done, is now running his own label as well, he's involved with a lot of people.

A lot of people involved with the group are involved with other things, for instance Paul Smith with Blast First, and Amrik Rai with Fon. Do you think that in some ways detracts from what you do? Would it be better if you had someone that was concentrating on your promotion 100% of the time?

Richard: That's a situation I would prefer, but unfortunately it's difficult to find someone. The way a lot of people seem to organise things these days is by setting up management organisations and they tend to deal with several different groups.

Some sources have indicated that the finances of the group aren't as healthy as they were. Have you run into some tax problems?

Richard: We spent a lot of money on equipment – and bad accounting from the past has caught up with us. We are beginning to get that sorted out.

What happened? Were you relying too heavily on an accountant?

Richard: We had an accountant in Sheffield, who was OK up to a point – it was OK but it got a bit out of hand. He was unable to deal with it – I don't want to go into too much detail about it.

Is it irreparable?

Richard: No, I wouldn't have thought so. There is the possibility of selling the studio, which is coming more and more of a reality as time goes on. But with the circumstances we are in at the moment that would make very little difference because EMI pay for all the recording, so they're quite happy to put us in a studio. We were the exception to the rule, I don't think there is any other group that uses their own set up.

You're used to taking a fairly long time building up your material in your own studio. Do you think that the material would change if you started recording LPs in 2 weeks?

Richard: I'm against the idea of getting rid of our own studio, but I'm for the idea of going into another studio with a blank sheet of paper so to speak. I think it would be interesting. 'The Crackdown' album was done in that way. We went into the studio with half an idea and recorded an album in four days. I think the next recording that is done might include a third party – a producer or someone to bounce ideas off. I think there needs to be someone else there. When you work with someone for so long it can get a bit jaded. A fresh input from people is welcome.

The roles do seem to have become extremely polarised. Do you think there is a danger of becoming too insular?

Richard: Yeah. Also working with the same equipment. I would like the idea of maybe going into a Fairlight studio and actually just working from scratch there – actually building things up in a computer to see what can be done that way. I like the idea of a new paintbox of sound, so to speak, it appeals to me.

What about the development of the video side. The 'Don't Argue' video must have been very expensive I would imagine. Do you think you can carry on being funded to make those sorts of videos without chart success?

Richard: Well, when we first went to EMI there was talk of doing a long form of video, but I think that's just been shoved to one side. I don't know whether it will happen or not.

The last time we spoke we discussed the possible making of a film. The footage that you started for that eventually ended up on the 'Gasoline In Your Eye' video. Do you think that a film or long video is unworkable in the pop format?

Richard: Yeah. If you're highly successful then I think you can talk to people on your own terms, because the people that fund those sorts of things know, that because of a certain name person being involved, then people are going to be interested in it even if it is not a string of promos. But I think in our position at the moment it is difficult. It would be quite easy to turn out another 'Gasoline In Your Eye' but what's the point? Without quite a lot of financial backing I couldn't really see anything good coming out of a thing like that.

Godley and Creme have just started a project that is attempting to take video out of the promo mould and into an artform in itself. Do you think that could be successful?

Richard: We were actually involved in that when it first got going. We thought we were going to be funded along with Pete Care to do a 25 minute piece, which we wrote and went ahead and approached J.G. Ballard with a view to him writing 3 or 4 minutes of some kind of scenario. To take maybe 10 themes and intercut the whole thing together but in the end they just backed out and the whole thing fell apart. But as regards the question, it depends on what people they approach I suppose.

The later videos like 'Sensoria' and 'Don't Argue' have used a Director and taken more of a 'plot' format and featured less of the cut-up imagery. Have you moved on from that?

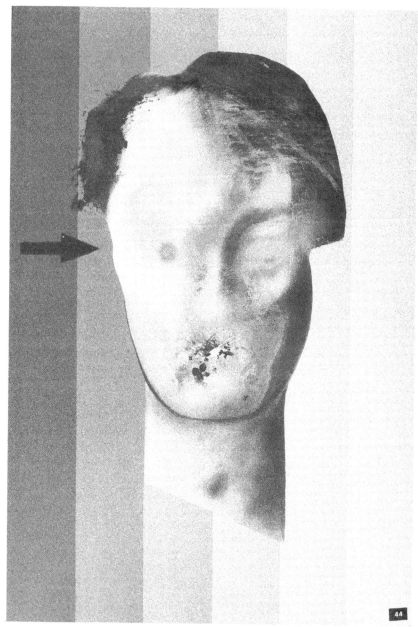

"The Enigma of Richard H. Kirk" (painting by Geoff Spiers)

Richard: You might think that it is more of a plot format but try telling that to someone at a TV station! Their concept of a pop video is some flashing lights and a few people dancing, you know. I don't know whether it's our name or our reputation or what, but no one in England would show those videos – the recent ones.

Why was that?

Richard: Well, no one would be specific. Maybe they just think they're crap videos. Maybe it's the ideas and the imagery.

Didn't EMI exert quite a lot of pressure to get them shown?

Richard: I mean, I'm not really sure as to what goes on to get things done – who pays who or what. As far as I know they tried to get the things shown. They've not been a problem out of England. In Europe they've been shown and in the States.

There does seem to be a very moral tone around at the moment in England – probably partly as a backlash to AIDS. A lot of people are beginning to feel they are being hampered in expressing themselves artistically.

Richard: A lot of people in the TV companies seem to set themselves up as some kind of moral guardian for the Nation's youth if you like. While things like that are going on it doesn't leave much hope. Even chart groups get problems with stuff – get asked to take bits of things out. I mean it's quite a dilemma with what to do, and say, "Right, we're not going to take anything out", and then no one gets to see it apart from a few of your mates.

With the resurgence of a moral tone, some people argue that it has proved that the '60s permissive society has turned in on itself. Or is there still some mileage to be made out of it?

Richard: It is really difficult to know where things are going in that respect.

However, I think it would be difficult to imagine someone like Warhol, even with his ability to attract attention, starting out and making the films he did now.

Richard: Yeah, there are always going to be things like that in existence but it is going to be stuff that is kind of underground – it's going to be privately shown and done really cheaply. But Warhol had very little to do with his later films anyway. He put his name to it which was enough for him by that time – he'd put his name to anything.

Now that he's died what are your opinions about the man?

Richard: I still have admiration for him and respect for his work. I always did – it's always inspired me. In the end Andy Warhol just became the work. He was invited to the parties, he had his own TV show which is what he always wanted to do.

The success of Warhol always seemed to typify America to me. What are your opinions about the place now that you have been there more often?

Richard: I like the place. I could get to like New York but I don't think I could live there because it's too difficult to get some peace and quiet. I mean if you're stuck in the middle of Manhattan, there is so much going on – when do you stop? (laughs)

If your success grew out there you would consider living out there part of the time?

Richard: Yes, I would welcome something like that, I'd be quite happy for a change of environment basically. I'd like the idea of actually going and working there, whether it would be recording or anything else – just getting a different sort of stimulus and different surroundings.

What is your favourite type of music at the moment? What have you been listening to?

Richard: I've started listening to Can again quite a lot. A lot of black music – or dance music – but not the kind of soul stuff. But the sort of stuff that I believe to be where the forefront of experimental music is at this point in time.

Do you think that white English people can produce that kind of music or is it primarily a black American phenomenon?

Richard: No, I don't think it is. I think basically there's a lot of snobbery involved. It is interesting that you find that groups from England or Europe can actually become part of the nightclub thing in New York. They seem to like it over there, whereas over here it has got to be American. The MARRS record proved that to be exactly what it is – it's snobbery. That record's initial success came because people assumed it was an American import.

Quite a lot of your contemporaries, like New Order, have moved towards the dance vein with considerable success, do you think that is because they structure their material more as songs rather than pieces of music?

Richard: I think a lot of New Order's work has always been fairly song-structured to me. With them you're dealing with a band. The comparisons between us and them aren't that large, apart from the fact that we started working around the same time. We probably don't work in any remotely similar way.

You've always stressed two things – firstly that you don't write songs and secondly that you don't class yourselves as musicians. Have either of those views changed?

Richard: I wouldn't know how to go about writing a song as such, but having said that, using technology it is possible to create structures which people would identify with as being songs.

What about your view of not being a musician. A lot of people might take that with a bit of cynicism seeing the type of material you have been producing and the length of time you have been producing it?

Richard: I still don't consider myself to be a musician. I can't write music as such. Still one of the main compositional tools that I favour is the multi track tape. Given the technology available anyone can be a musician these days anyway. It's no problem anymore.

Everything in terms of music in the '80's has become very mainstream. Might there be a turn around to the more independent scene, or do you think that is well and truly redundant now?

Richard: It's by no means redundant because there's still a lot of people out there who have got this notion that they'll only go out and buy things if it's on an independent label. I'm sure there's a lot of people around who are still of that view. That's probably affected us after we've been seen to go to the 10th major corporation in the world or whatever. It might upset a few of your die-hards!

I can understand all too well why it would appeal to a lot of people to go from an independent label to a major. If you've been making music for two or three years and you're still signing on the dole or penniless all the time, then I can understand people getting pissed off with that situation, looking elsewhere and doing something about it. As it happens that didn't particularly affect us – with us only being two or three in the group we managed ably financially when we were with an independent label – you had to wait maybe a little bit longer to get royalty payments. I can see that side of it. The frightening side of it is that you get so many people now that are willing to run forward and be exploited and not even question the whole thing. That disturbs me.

Looking to the future, how long do you think you will continue doing what you are doing now without having a hit or major success?

Richard: I don't know, it's difficult to say. I wouldn't have thought for that much longer. I think at some point in time you have to say, "Right, lets put this thing to rest and move on to something different", or on the other hand try and become even more cynical and go for even more mainstream success. We have done everything else, you know what I mean? (laughs)

Critics might say that the Cabaret Voltaire bandwagon has run its course.

Richard: Yeah, I'm sure they would. A lot of them have said so in print as well! (laughs) I mean, I think a lot of people are cynical – I think they take what we do for granted because we've been around for so long and they think, "Oh, yeah it's another Cabaret Voltaire record". I think in terms of the music press, the people who review our records are from a different generation to us. It's bound to happen where it's the thing to do to have a go at people who have been in existence for a long time – but personally I think they've picked on the wrong people, because as far as I'm concerned we're still as credible as we ever were. I don't think they are justified in having a go at us.

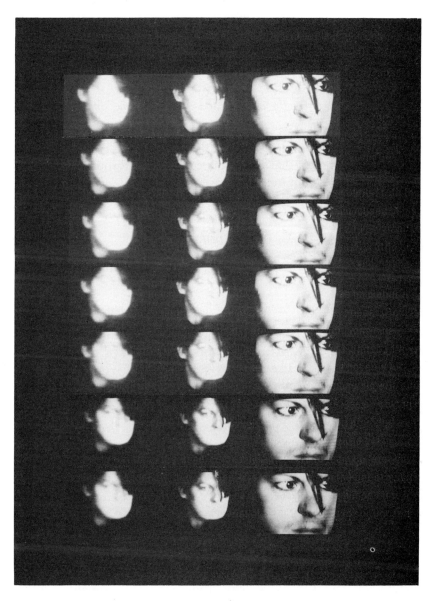

Richard H. Kirk, who one reviewer once described as, "The world's most paranoid man".

Who do you think comprises your audience now?

Richard: I don't know, there again I've never known anyway. I mean it's difficult to judge – that is one thing about not playing live for a couple of years – at least you did have some contact with people at concerts.

Do you think you've finally managed to lay the 'long mac' image to rest?

Richard: No, that's still there. As I've said before, when you do interviews people still see us as the indie group that went to a major label. I mean there's that magazine called Underground that deals just with independent music and we're still in that – I mean I'm not knocking the magazine, I think it's quite good – it's just a bit strange.

Do you think you will ever shake off that tag?

Richard: Yeah, by having a mega hit single. Maybe then it might hit home.

Do you think that is any closer than it was three years ago?

Richard: Yeah, maybe – maybe not. If it happens it might not be here – more feasibly it might happen in America or Europe or somewhere. I would like that anyway because it would mean that the radio over here couldn't ignore it which would be quite a good situation to be in.

If that were to happen the pressure to promote and play live would be more prominent. Would you respond to that pressure?

Richard: The pressure to do that is there now, but I'm not actually sure whether playing live sells records.

It must be a good way of making money though?

Richard: It always has done in the past. But I remember reading that it was only really the stadium bands that made the real money – and they were all established bands. It is a way of making money and it's separate from any income from the record company. A lot of bands do go out for a cynical reason – you find out that a lot of tours are just set up because someone has just got a tax bill. You find out things like that as you go along.

With Mal living in London, increasingly more and more so, have you found that it is more difficult to work on things now?

Richard: Not really, I've a lot of the time been left to my own devices, which I don't mind – I'm quite happy to get on with that. But as I say it is a good time to actually try a different approach – I'm all for that. That would probably involve me travelling to London more – working in a studio.

Basically, Western Works had to close, was that the scenario?

Richard: Yeah, the building was falling apart and someone broke a big hole through the roof and tried to take all the equipment away with them. At the moment we've moved to a new studio which is a lot bigger – and a lot more expensive. (laughs) It actually resembles a studio more than Western Works did.

So, you have carried on buying more and more equipment.

Richard: Yeah, the other problem with that is that is not allowable as it used to be for tax purposes. You only get a very small proportion of it – whilst 5 or 6 years ago you'd see an accountant and he'd say, "Yeah, go ahead spend all your money on equipment", which is what we did. But 5 years later you find that isn't the case. The other thing to bear in mind these days is that 8 track or 16 track equipment is far better than it ever used to be six years ago. There's one 16 track available now that's better than the 24 track we've got. If we sell the studio I'll get a smaller set up just for composing things at home. Which I don't mind.

Lyn: But I do!

What about your interests outside music are they still much the same? Do you still enjoy the same type of literature, same type of movies?

Richard: Yeah, the same old rubbish. (laughs)

You haven't discovered any new obsessions apart from the old tried and tested? Would you still say that your obsessions were firearms, kitsch and pornography?

Richard: Yeah, still of interest – obsession might be too strong a word.

Might you end up like Burroughs with his collection of firearms?

Richard: I don't know, I don't know whether I'll live that long. (laughs) It's funny because it's only now that he's getting the recognition – a few years back you couldn't have imagined someone like that getting on the front cover of the Sunday Times magazine. Now he's been claimed as America's greatest writer.

Although the TV media never seems to accept things like that. For instance it seems ironic to me that someone like Genet can die with little or no coverage whilst 5 hours or whatever gets allotted to an appreciation of Eammon Andrews merely because he was a TV personality. Do you think that to be respected in this day and age you have to be a TV personality?

Richard: I mean the TV is where the majority of people seem to get their information from these days – TV is the one still. Although cinema is making a big come back over the last few years – a lot of people seem to be actually going out and seeing more films.

Lyn: Yeah, but they're all going to see 'Top Gun'.

So is the media still crap?

Richard: Yeah, it's still crap but I'm still fascinated by it for all its crapness. It will be quite interesting when the thing opens up with cable TV – you know, who'll they'll let have a programme. They'll probably keep it really controlled.

Not like in Amsterdam where the cable TV is either pornography or religious broadcasts.

Richard: I can't see religious TV being that big over here like it is in America, somehow I just can't see it.

What are some of the films and books you have enjoyed recently?

Richard: 'Blue Velvet' like everyone else. 'Robocop'. There's a couple of Ballard books I've read recently, the Kray Twins 'A Profession of Violence' is a good little read.

The whole notion of violence still fascinates you. You still like watching all the gory films.

Richard: Yeah, splatter. I mean it's just ridiculous the extent to which some of the videos now go.

Lyn: It doesn't affect you anymore – it's like eating chips or something.

Do you not get bored with them? It's like with porno movies, people say after you've seen the umpteenth one you get to the point of saying, "So what".

Richard: I must admit I tend to check out a lot of Hollywood films as well now. I don't bother to go to the cinema to see them, I'm not that interested, but just to get to see 'Top Gun' and things like that – stuff that is really successful – I watch them because I want to know why people go to see them.

Do you still think most of them are crap though?

Richard: Yeah, if at least you take the time to see these things at least you can justify saying that. It interests me what appeals to the masses.

Personally, I am more interested in European films, they seem to take a totally different approach to that of Hollywood.

Lyn: People don't want to know what you think. (laughs)

Richard: Neither do they want to know what you think. (laughs)

Do you still keep in touch with Chris Watson?

Richard: Yes, he's sometimes a difficult man to track down. He was in the South of England for quite a while working for the RSPB and I posted him some records and there was a delay of some two months until I heard from him – the letter came from Newcastle and apparently he'd got sick of it down there and decided to move back to Newcastle.

The Hafler Trio in some respects have carried on the idea of sound experimentation in a purer form. Do you think in still doing that they are barking up the wrong tree?

Richard: No, I don't – I still respect Chris tremendously for what he's doing. I'm not saying that I would want to that myself but I think what he does is extremely valid.

However, those types of groups who were doing that sort of sound experimentation were very much a thing of the late '70s and early '80s – what became to be known as the 'industrial tag'.

Richard: That 'industrial tag' was never something we particularly encouraged. It's was the tag people used.

So, your connections with some of those groups, Psychic TV for example, have become less over the years.

Richard: I think, of the people that were working at that time – you can't expect everyone to be working in eachother's pockets and remain the same. Everyone diversifies. But that is not to say that we've severed contact with these people – I'm still quite happy to speak to all those people. It's just I very rarely bump into them these days. A lot of that is probably to do with my geographical location more than anything else.

Do you often think that maybe you're the last of your contemporaries who are still going, that haven't had major chart success. People like The Cure, Echo and the Bunnymen....

Richard: Yeah, but I wouldn't associate myself with those types of groups. What they were doing was completely different – I mean that was purely a musical thing.

What about New Order and The Fall?

Richard: I can't speak for The Fall – but just looking back at what we've left behind if you like, it's not just a bunch of records. There's a lot of other things as well.

Richard adopts a charismatic stare in a rare solo photograph.

THE ART OF THE SIXTH SENSE

Say the records didn't sell or the group split up completely, would it be the visual media you would move into do you think?

Richard: I think I will always be interested in that and I always want to do something. But it is just a case of not wanting to repeat oneself given a limited budget.

Do you get many offers to do anything of that nature, or production?

Richard: Visually I don't think there's been anything – that's more difficult because our main collaborator Pete Care lives in Los Angeles so it is a bit difficult to discuss your ideas without building up a massive transatlantic phone bill.

The 'Sensoria' video won the Los Angeles Times video award. Is that right?

Richard: Yeah, it's also in the Museum of Modern Art so there must be something to it.

Do you think that 'Sensoria' has been your most successful record to date?

Richard: No. 'Nag Nag Nag'. (laughs) I don't really know. I mean 'Sensoria' never got an American release, if it had that could probably have done a lot more. I mean it's still feasible that it might be re-released at some time.

Some of your most successful records have been those that have been re-mixed. Do you think that says something about the way that you record?

Richard: Yeah, I think the most successful records we've ever done in terms of sales have been done with producers – whether it is true artistically I don't know.

Does that not beg the question of whether a fully recorded and produced record is not the best step forward?

Richard: Well, we've really already done that. When I say that we've had people come in and re-mix the stuff, we've worked with people like Adrian Sherwood and John Robie – but the idea has always been there, not finished but semi-completed. If we actually set something up from zero, it would be quite interesting to see where it ended up – it might end up with complete chaos and violence. (laughs) But on the other hand it might be something that is really good.

Certainly the added touches to the single of 'Sensoria' seemed to liven it up from the original LP track.

Richard: It was two tracks edited together on multi-track, literally just cut together – which I suppose was a bit ahead of its time again, so much as that is how people tend to make records these days – a lot of dance music now consists of different tracks just glued together – cemented with a few different beats.

Do you think that EMI signed you on the strength of 'Sensoria'?

Richard: That and 'I Want You' – I think they saw a lot of pop potential in there. We're not as big a gamble as people would actually think. Companies like EMI sign up a lot of groups, spend about 5 times as much money on them as they have on us, and they sell about 2,000 records. But when they signed us, the whole thing was presented by Amrik in terms that business affairs people could understand. "This is the amount of records the group sells... etc. They're not just a group, they do audio-visual stuff as well".

How do Amrik and Stevo compare as managers?

Richard: I'd decline to comment on that one actually. At least not in print anyway. They have such different musical tastes you just can't begin to compare them. They're two different kettles of fish altogether.

But a manager of some kind is essential?

Richard: Yeah, I think if you're dealing with major labels and operating on that kind of level, I think they expect there to be a manager there. I think it freaks them out if they have to deal direct with the group.

I heard Dave Gahan from Depeche Mode recently saying on the radio that they do a lot of the day to day running of the group, setting up tours etc.

Richard: I'd be very sceptical about that. I'm sure they have people who organise it for them. I mean, we used to set up tours, I used to do a hell of a lot of that type of work – ringing people up and haggling over the price and the riders. I quite enjoyed it actually – but there comes a time when you think, "Fuck it, I don't want to be doing this all the time – this isn't my job, I want to concentrate on recording". I think you have to be able to delegate things to other people – you can't clone yourself – at least not yet. (laughs)

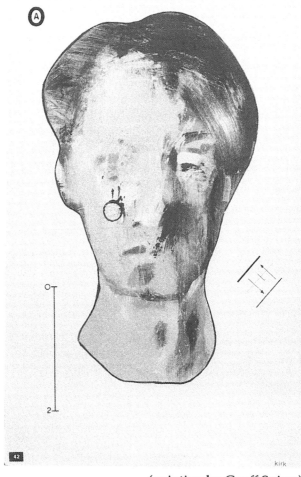

(painting by Geoff Spiers)

stephen
mallinder

STEPHEN MALLINDER

Stephen Mallinder, known to all as 'Mal', is these days somewhat of a debonair socialite, and as such is now by definition London-based – as has nearly always been dictated by the confines of the 'music business' in England. A vegetarian with a likeable line in chatter, he is both a follower of soap operas as well as the chic or hip, he has often represented the fashionable and accessible side of Cabaret Voltaire.

He was always one of the possible contenders in the early '80s for Brian Ferry's vacant crown, so much so that Paul Morley once daubed him in an NME column as "The best looking man in rock". However, there was no one, Mallinder included, that was able to become that self-style orientated to take on Ferry's mantle, with the possible exception of David Sylvian. Morley also once mused in his pseudo column Errol that he was convinced that Mal and Sylvian were having an affair. A piece of homo-erotic silliness with little credibility.

Early Roxy Music was an obvious and larger influence on Cabaret Voltaire, and Mallinder in particular, than would first appear. Roxy's sense of style combined with 'experimentalist' tendencies must have seemed at the time both slightly surreal but also tinged with and tempered by 'pop' elements. Ferry and Eno were not only to dress in outrageous costumes but also to dress their music with odd synthesiser noises and tape recorded sound. There was an obvious humourous side to Roxy Music's glam posturings that provided a perfect foil and accompiment to Bowie's more camp (Kemp) presentation at that time. Eno and Bowie were to team up later on Bowie's Lps 'Low' and 'Heroes' to produce some of the finest music of the late '70s. However, Eno as a musician backed himself into a corner becoming a quasi-theorist of the avant garde in sound, and

Bowie returned to the mainstream with increasingly less adventurous LPs.

The choice was open to Cabaret Voltaire to follow either of these paths, but as ever they sat somewhere in the middle. They had always divorced themselves from both the avant garde and the mainstream, but the bright lights of the latter seemed to beckon more invitingly particularly to Mallinder. Retrospectively it is probably fair to say that Mallinder was always more of the potential pop star than the sound experimentalist. A continuing and increasing liking for soul and mainstream music became more evident than continuing a need to break down any musical barriers.

It may have been with that in mind that Mallinder, once the nagging bark of Cabaret Voltaire, turned to more soothing contortions of the throat. Gone were the threateningly military shouts of the early material to be replaced by a lilting coaxing from the microphone of something that could be approximated to singing. Lyrically the material remained as obscure and as unfathomable as ever. They rarely hinted at the person pushing the pen, and stood as stoically non-referential. Live, a harder edge still prevailed, the voice returned much more to its original intention of providing hoarse punctuation to the backing tracks. On stage he became the focus for what little activity there was – as the group started to step out of the shadow of their back projections.

Mallinder has always been much more vocal than Kirk – and therefore became the natural mouthpiece for the group, especially after they became a duo. He is also much more open to criticism of the group's music, particularly some of the older material. His position seems to be to regard it as a natural learning process (warts and all) to arrive at the position they had reached. Latterly, Mallinder's role within the group appeared to be more and more as vocalist, spokesman, and general man about town, doing what had to be done to retain the group's position in the pop music field.

Any pressure this newly assumed role might have exerted only appeared to affect him once, when in New York after a gruelling set of interviews, under his own admission he threw what could be termed a wobbler. After so long a time to wait to debut in New York, usually the first port of call for any up and coming English band, it would not be unfair to say that Cabaret Voltaire and New York viewed each other as mutually anti-climactic.

Once the owner of a house in Sheffield, he now prefers to live in London. It might be fair to say that there came a time when he and quite a few others in a similar position felt they had outgrown their localised environment – in Mallinder's case, Sheffield. Although the cynical might purport that there were more nightclubs and free drinks to be had in London, to fit in with Mallinder's hedonistic lifestyle. However, it was undoubtedly true that much of the powerful focus that had centred around the North in places like Sheffield and Manchester in the early '80s had dissipated. The Halcyon days with the likes of The Human League had faded, and as the eighties drew on there was a feeling that, similar to employment in general, if you wanted to get on, go South.

What have been your main changes in attitude in the three years since we last spoke?

Mal: I think since then I have become slightly less serious about it. It's really difficult because you don't go into the studio and think, "Oh, my attitude's changed"... (pause) I don't suppose it has changed that much apart from a slightly more frivolous approach with which I want to do it now. Having stopped working for a few months and having the chance to look at other people, both on major labels and independent ones – because I see both sides – it's amazing how serious they have got about it all, either musically serious or artistically serious. I don't think anyone really started off like that – in the punk days it was never that serious. I think I've started to take it a bit more tongue-in-cheek. I still take what I do seriously – but not the end result.

In terms of recording, we've done two albums since then. One was 'The Covenant' where we went back to basics and did it all in our own studio in Sheffield – and then there is the first EMI album, 'Code'.

You mention going back to basics, presumably referring to the fact that 'The Crackdown' was recorded in a studio in London. Do you think that you took a step backwards in recording subsequent material in your own studio and as a result of that the material has suffered?

Mal: Yeah, I think so. For me personally we didn't make the best of the position we were in. I think there was a danger, looking back, that Cabaret Voltaire had very much become a sacred cow – which is where Richard and I differed – and I got fed up with becoming the sacred cow that we must respect and had to represent something. Whereas really it didn't, because what people thought it meant in 1978/9 had gradually been eroded away – rather than it being a case of saying, "Oh, it doesn't mean that anymore, it's changed to this". The music had gradually changed, it had become more mainstream – which was intentional. But at the same time there was this horrible, "It has to represent something" – which is true to a certain degree but I don't know why we should have been so respectful of it anyway.

In the first stages we were tongue-in-cheek, we were dadaist in our attitude towards it, so regarding this name, this anonymous entity that was Cabaret Voltaire, with ultimate respect was ironic. I think we held it in too much esteem, so when we were going back to doing recordings in our own studio, and when we were writing with Adrian Sherwood, we were holding ourselves back a little. Whereas we were in the position where people were saying, "Well, you've achieved everything else, why don't you do this, why don't you do that?" – because people knew what we stood for, it wouldn't make any difference what music we made, because we'd established those things in the first place so there is no need necessarily to hold true to them.

It sounds to me as if you are saying that you should have launched yourselves more into becoming a 'pop' band.

Mal: Yeah, I think that's true. It's partly true about the music, but I think it's more true in terms of the way that we presented ourselves. I think that was the downfall with the last EMI album – which was a lot more listenable even though it has got the elements that we held true to – but people still saw us as two distant people, one standing behind the other.

Were you selling yourselves in the wrong way?

Mal: Yeah, I think so really. The records would have warranted being sold in a different way. I think now my attitude is that it's more appealing, more interesting and more valid, to make tough records but actually present yourself in a ridiculous way – than actually do safe records and present it in a very tough way. The music is the important thing and not the personality behind it. The pop medium treats personalities as a joke anyway, so you might as well take the piss out of yourself because they're going to take the piss out of you anyway. So, I think over the last two years we shouldn't have presented ourselves as seriously – as I've already said that is where Richard and I differ, because Richard does have this self-respect, which is fair enough, but there is also a danger of becoming caricature of yourself.

Do you think you moving to London had anything to do with your change in attitude?

Mal: I didn't move to London to get away from being regarded as part of that Northern industrial funk sort of thing – but it was purely by chance – partly because of my then girlfriend Karen – and partly because I wanted to get away from Sheffield because I felt it was more valid – and it has been. Although Richard would probably think that I deserted Sheffield. In a lot of respects I've managed to achieve a lot more for the group being in London because it has meant that I'm a lot more available – I can do interviews, I can do things on spec that I couldn't have done otherwise. So, it has been helpful although I didn't come for those reasons, I came for personal reasons.

London has had a very good effect on me in the fact that when you move to London you realise that you are a very small fish in a big pond, whereas in Sheffield I was a big fish in a very small pond, and you tend to get a rather perverted view of your own worth, esteem or position. I realised, when even up to a year ago and I used to go in to places like The Leadmill (a club in Sheffield) people would recognise you – but really that means fuck all. So, moving down to London did actually deflate my ego, but for me it had a beneficial effect because it put it more in perspective.

Would it be right to surmise that some of the major differences of opinion of late have been over promotion and playing live?

Mal: That is where Richard and I differed because we wanted to do it on different terms. Richard wanted to do it on his terms, which is doing very selective dates – which is fine and was OK ten years ago. But particularly abroad, if you want to do something you have to play a number of dates. It's fine if you're the Pet Shop Boys, then you can get by without actually doing gigs – but the point is they do the equivalent of gigs as they're out of the country all the time doing promotion. Their actual image and the way they present themselves lends itself to TV, video and to all the interviews and all that. For us we have to go about it in a round-about way because people view us in a certain way – so therefore if you're going to play live then you've got to do it quite intensively.

Also, there's the finances of it. The last time we played America we did a selective number of dates – took it easy – and we actually lost money on it. So, I respect that Richard doesn't regard promotion as his area – that's fine to a point but because he was part of the group it meant that there were certain things that were demanded of him. For instance, about three months ago, we were supposed to go to Greece to do two TV appearances and Richard said that he couldn't be bothered to go – which is not very healthy when there's only two of you in the group.

Many of the records in the charts at the moment use similar features to yours, found voices over a funk backing track. Why do you think you have been unable to corner any of that commercial success?

Mal: Because I think we used those features in a different way – we opened the door for a lot of people to be able to use those things. But those people are using it in a more accessible but somewhat more gimmicky way. I think that's why the public are far more open to the 'Bomb the Bass' record or the 'Pump up the Volume' record – it's just done in a more palatable way – that's all. I think we used it in a more upfront, challenging way – and they use it in a more musical, restrained way.

Do you think you are incapable of making commercial music?

Mal: I don't think that either of us have that make up – that doesn't mean that we couldn't do it – it's just that from what I know now I realise there's a certain craft or subtlety involved. That's why I've found using producers useful because they can actually use those elements to better ends and a better effect – whilst we use them in maybe a cruder way. We have the bass line, rhythm track, string line, but there is an actual skill and a craft in putting that together and we haven't actually achieved that in the past – there's been hints and suggestions of it – but there's always been the fact that if there had been that extra input, that extra nurturing of those elements then I think it would work. I don't think it has been totally absent – there have been catchy things in our stuff but I think maybe it's always needed an outside view of it – that's all.

Might the missing element just be that of sitting down and writing a song, like say New Order do, rather than a piece of music?

Mal: I think New Order are much more musical in their approach. Also, there's an inter-communication because they are a group. With two people, the system has very much been Richard working on the music, me doing the vocals – and when they gel they gel, and when they don't it's tough shit. I think a lot of it is the inter-relation between myself and Richard, which needed that outside thing – because you know what Richard's like, he's very single-minded about the way that he wants to work, but it has probably always needed an extra person if it was supposed to have that extra added 'poppier' aspect to it.

Do you think you have been hampered by sticking to some of the statements you have traditionally made, such as, "We're not musicians". Some people might view that with a certain amount of cynicism.

Mal: Yes, it's a classic line, it just means that you're not a trained musician. It's bullshit to say that in doing this for ten years we haven't learnt a certain degree of musicality. And also, you know what's in tune, what's out of tune, you know when you're coming in on the wrong beat – therefore the point is that it's almost admitting the rules are there and tying yourself to them, but not using them to their proper effect – which we were starting to do on the last album. But, yes it's held us back – that goes back to the notion of this 'sacred cow' aspect of the group, which is the fear of doing it, whereas we should just fucking let loose and do it.

You have also had some financial problems recently, were you just naive in letting that side of it get out of hand?

Mal: I think it is a two way thing. Yes, I think we were very naive and we trusted the wrong people in terms of our accounts – not management but accountants. I think it was purely that we were lulled into a false sense of security. We were naive – and also man can not live by advances alone, you can't do it – so it was bound to catch up on us.

Do you think the fact that a lot of the people involved with the group are doing other things has been to the detriment of the group?

Mal: It would be nice to say that we have a manager that handles us all the time – 100%. But we don't actually do enough work to warrant that – no one could live on just working for us. If we were touring a lot it would be different.

Your videos have been quite widely critically acclaimed, but again not shown to a great degree. Is that still a basic underlying uncommerciality?

Mal: I think it's our name – full stop. I think the name actually puts a block on certain things – radio play, video play. I don't think the content of the videos themselves actually stops them from being shown, just as the records don't stop themselves from being played. But I think because of the way we presented ourselves there is a

very stand off attitude towards them. I think videos in general have actually spiralled inwards to a degree where the effect of a video now is very diminished. I don't think we could ever make another 'Sensoria' and I don't think anyone ever could – I thought that was a ground-breaking video. I don't think anyone could do it again and that's because everybody makes videos now and it has become less valid. I don't think the form itself is actually valid.

Godley and Creme have tried to take it out of its current genre and make it into an artform in itself.

Mal: I personally don't think it'll work. I admire them for doing it and I admire Godley and Creme immensely, I like their attitude, I think it's great. But the whole notion of video now as an artform has just disappeared and I don't know whether it has gone too far toward a commercial thing for people to pull back from it. I think the odd person will try and make an arty video – Sting or whoever – and that is probably as arty as you can probably get on mainstream TV. I'd like to think it would happen, but people have tried it so much and it doesn't work, because people expect certain things from video – people don't want art.

Is that a reflection on the '80s?

Mal: I think it's a reflection on the music business – I think it's a reflection on the records. I just mean in this climate I don't think it will change. I think the climate has got to change before anyone can make greater inroads into using video as an artform.

There seems to be a more restrictive attitude in this country – partly as a response to AIDS – do you think that hampers people expressing themselves visually in videos?

Mal: I think if you're big enough you can still express yourself any way you want. Nobody stopped George Michael smoking cigarettes in his last video – you're not supposed to, but he did. Nobody stopped him showing scantily clad women in the video – they stopped us, but that is because it is us, and not because of the scantily clad women.

Your biggest progress recently has been an increase in your popularity in America. Why do you think that is?

Mal: Because we didn't have records out there before, I think that's all it is. We'd been over to America and played two or three times, we'd had good press, the videos had been shown and we'd had good press for them, and I think people were aware of the name but had not been able to get the records – now they're able to get the records so our popularity has gone up. It's not been a massive increase but at least the records have been available. You could say that it was because of the dancibility of the records to a degree – but America is still very M.O.R. and A.O.R., it's not changed that much. But really it is down to changing from being a cult group where people couldn't get the records outside of LA and New York, to a situation where people can get the records a little bit more. There is an increase in awareness in the States that we've been able to capitalise on from having a release over there.

Perhaps you can start afresh over there and not be tied to that 'long mac' po-faced image?

Mal: I think that's true anywhere outside of England where they don't take that much notice of the NME and that sort of thing.

But also it's the only place where you've played live in the last two years. Is that because America appeals to you?

Mal: America still appeals to me, I still like America a lot. I still don't know whether I could live there but it does appeal to me. It's the basis of this popular culture that we're in now – so you might as well go and see it at its source. I mean, it revolts me, but it also attracts me at the same time?

What sort of music do you like listening to now?

Mal: Well, it's a bit of a cliche but it's still a lot of black dance music – a lot of the 'house' stuff, the 'acid house' stuff, the 'go-go' stuff, all that fascinates me.

Do you think that white people can successfully recreate that?

Mal: I think they can, because music is music, I don't think that colour matters anymore. A lot of that is image anyway, and the way that it's presented. On most black records there's more white people working on it than black people, so I don't think it makes that much difference. It's a bit awkward to answer because it actually brings out the latent snobbery in people – because if they listen to a record and they find out white people have made it and it's a very soulful or funky record, the tendency is not to like it. That's why you or I would probably not dream of buying a Simply Red record but we would buy a Bobby Womack record. It just brings out snobbery in people really, and I'm just as much a victim of that as anyone else. And that's because we all like to personally own music – and there's nothing wrong with that – people like to get the latest thing, it's just like collecting Dinky cars really. People always want new things, and it's the same with black music, people want it from its source. But that's coming from me talking in England where you can get Chicago records easier than you can in Chicago. (laughs)

How long do you think you can carry on with what you are doing at the moment without having any major success?

Mal: I wouldn't want to carry on much longer because I have become ambitious – I was always ambitious – but the longer you go on the more it aggravates you and the more you want to actually achieve a certain degree. It's not just financial success, or an ego thing, but you do want to achieve it – see some sort of physical reward for it, that sort of profile. So, therefore I don't really want to bring out records that I don't believe in 100% or that I don't think would be 100% successful anymore – because using things as an art statement is crap now and I think it was very much a mystery thing that we lived in for four years – everybody did. I still believe in my own credibility and I'm still an elitist in a lot of ways – I still think I'm better than anyone else. But having said that I want to make records that I'm proud of and that I think will be successful.

So, you still see that ambition taking the form of making records?

Mal: There's this horrible attitude when you get to a certain stage of making music, of wanting to be whisked off to the hinterlands of making soundtrack music – which is fine, it's a valid point but I

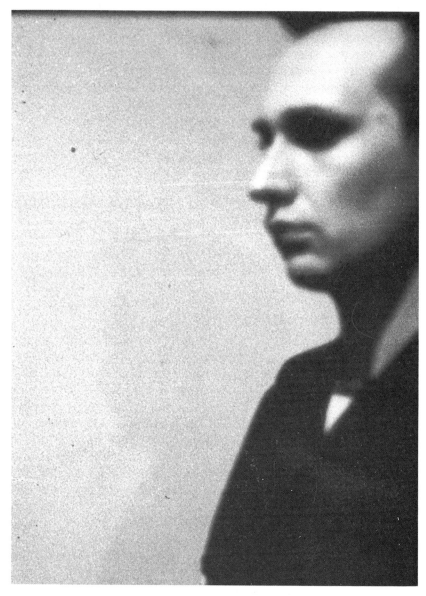

The profile of Mallinder, who Paul Morley once described as the best looking man in Rock.

wouldn't want to do that and nothing else. Because I wouldn't want to be that sort of person locked away doing soundtrack music. I mean it's wonderful if you're Enio Morricone or John Barry – the music they make is incredibly valid but that's a different sort of thing. I don't really want to see myself for the rest of my life making music for artforms. I would like to do it but I would also like to counterbalance it. That's the reason why I started making music in the first place and the reason why we stopped making music in a loft and why we started going out and playing and making records. There's a danger in this sort of fear of putting yourself public – hiding behind soundtrack music – things like that.

So you have always felt the most commercially minded of the group – even going way back to those days in the loft.

Mal: Well, obviously that stands out. I suppose it does go without saying. Chris did it for a certain reason, he left for a certain reason to go off and do other things. Richard doesn't want to be involved in the promotion side whereas I, whether I like it or not, see it as a valid part of it. It's like anything else – you have to take the shit with the good side of it. The good side of it is being able to go into studios and do the records you want, but you've got to actually take the crap side of it if you want to get somewhere. Which involves acting like a complete plonker in Milan. It's funny – it's sick.

The Milan incident refers to you dressing up as Father Christmas?

Mal: Fuck, who told you about that – did I tell you that? (laughs)

A bit of an own goal there, I think. Do you think the independent band ethic is a thing of the past?

Mal: I don't think it was ever particularly valid as an ethic, I think it has always paralleled the major labels. But that's the unique thing about the set up in England which I've been part of and been very proud of, because it was actually very valid at the time. But England is unique in that it does have a totally independent set-up that works alongside the majors and it's successful. But if they are successful it's because they play the games that everybody plays. They don't do it without making videos, they don't do it without getting records on the radio. Apart from some dance records, where there are back ways into the charts which records like 'Pump Up the Volume' have proved.

Do you not get a feeling with some of those records, 'Pump Up the Volume' in particular, that you have been caught up and overtaken?

Mal: I think we were always caught up and overtaken anyway. Because with the things that we have done in the past there have been people working on the same ideas that we were a part of – not that we weren't innovative but we weren't that original. I've never seen ourselves as carrying the flag for something and now all of a sudden everybody's run past us. I don't think it makes any difference – I mean people were saying that to us four years ago, "Aren't you pissed off because so-and-so has got into the charts, because you were doing that two years ago", people have always been saying that about us. That's nobody's fault but our own, because if you want to capitalise on it you can do – it depends if you want to, really.

Certainly it is true that of all the groups that started around the same time as you, most of them have either had some chart success or split up.

Mal: Yeah, it's true. But they probably knew what they wanted a little bit more, we never knew particularly what we wanted – or at least maybe the realisation of it was that Richard and I want different things. I don't know.

One reviewer picked up on this when reviewing the first edition of this book by saying something on the lines of, "200 pages of interviews with two people who haven't a clue what they are doing".

Mal: It's true. But there again I fucking challenge anyone who does know exactly what they do. That's why I've become a lot more cynical and tongue-in-cheek about what I do – now I see people and their so fucking serious about what they do. I see this real musicianship thing from people that if they'd have carried on like that in the punk days they would have been beaten up for it – so I don't see why I should fall into that trap.

Isn't that true of most people though – that they end up doing what they started off attacking?

Mal: Yeah, well I'm doing what I started off attacking. But the difference is that I don't see that I should have to defend what I do as so fucking phenomenally important. You're as good as your next record – and a record is just an idea that goes on to tape and it's nothing more than that – it's nothing that's going to fucking change the world. If you've got belief in an idea then you follow it through in what ever way you can – and if it takes something to do it – then you fucking do it.

That's a more mercenary approach than I've heard from you before. It's a bit of a new attitude?

Mal: I know it is. But there again I didn't want to stay the same. I'm sure when you interviewed me three years ago my attitude was different from when 'Nag, Nag, Nag' came out. Nobody should be so set in their ways. I'm not a fundamentalist – or like these die hard Marxists – you have to adapt your ideals in what you do. Yeah, I know I've changed – but the world's changed as well. (laughs)

Without sounding cruel, it does sound a bit like the footballer at the end of his career who has suddenly decided he wants to score goals.

Mal: Yeah, probably. No not really, because as you say I was always the more commercially minded of us.

You were always a goal hanger!

Mal: Yeah I was always a shit liner. (laughs) I was always a bit of a Gary Lineker. It's true. A lot of it is because that role was hoist upon me because I was the singer. I was aware that I was in the position of being able to sell the records. When you've spent the last six months promoting a record like I have done for the last two singles and the last album it would be pretty pathetic if I didn't believe in my ability to promote records.

Will there be many more Cabaret Voltaire records?

Mal: And if there are, who will be on them. (laughs)

Neither of you. Chris Watson?

After only moderate success with his solo project Love Street,
Mallinder's thoughts returned to recording with Cabaret Voltaire.

Mal: Actually, neither of us own the name – EMI own the name Cabaret Voltaire.

So perhaps someone else could tour as you?

Mal: Oh, yeah. But seriously, that is a bone of contention at the moment – I don't really want to tour but I'm getting pressured to do dates. Richard doesn't really want to do dates – and if he does it is only four of five at a time. With things as they are at the moment, I don't really want to tour – just because of personal reasons really.

I understand that one of the possibilities at the moment is selling the studio? Although that decision to do so would presumably affect Richard more than you?

Mal: The thing is with Richard is that it is his lifeline because if you take the studio away – not being nasty – but he doesn't have a reason to carry on. The reason he's in Sheffield is because of the studio. Whereas I've been in the position for quite some time where I've had to book studio time if I want to record solo material. Which is a bit silly when we have our own studio – but the thing is Richard's grown up with it so much that it has become his studio and I can't just say I'm coming in to record and I'll be there for two weeks. I would feel odd doing it. But may be it would be good for Richard for us not to have the studio – it would always have been good for the group over the last two years if we hadn't had our own studio because it would've put us in the position of having to do it another way.

What about your interests outside of music?

Mal: What do I do when it gets dark. (laughs)

Yeah, how do you spend these long winter evenings? (laughs)

Mal: I have the same interests I always had – which is reading, going to see films. I haven't got a video, so I don't watch videos anymore – which is a bit ironic when I'm the Director of two video companies and I haven't got a video machine.

What sort of books have you enjoyed recently?

Mal: Nothing incredibly unusual really. I've gone back to reading a lot of Dashiell Hammett and Patricia Highsmith books – things like that. I'm reading 'An Interview with a Vampire' by Ann Rice at the moment, that's really good. Actually it's a bit like this – only it's set in current day San Francisco and there's this kid doing a fanzine interview with a vampire that's 200 years old.

It's very like this actually – I'm the kid and you're the vampire. (laughs)

Mal: Alright (laughs). As for films (pause) – 'Robocop' was wicked. 'Withnail and I' was good.

Would you say that your interests have become more mainstream as well – getting away from the initial influences like Burroughs?

Mal: Burroughs' books have become more mainstream. (laughs) No, I still look for things – I'm still interested in that sort of thing. But as you get older you're bound to ... God, I've gone middle class and middle aged – shit. (laughs) But what's on offer these days is more mainstream. I mean if you go to an art film I can give you 10 to 1 that it's at least 10 years old. Unless it's Derek Jarman and he does mostly videos now.

What about your video company, Doublevision? Is that dead or dormant?

Mal: I would say pretty dead, actually. It's not fair for me or Richard to say whether it's dead or whatever, because we became less part of it, we let Paul take over – and now Paul has got other interests, so we can't really say whether Doublevision is alive or not. It had to take a back seat for us because we were on Virgin and EMI. Also, if Doublevision is dead, all the other video labels that were around at the same time are dead as well because there isn't that sort of thing coming through. It goes back to what I was saying about the art films. A lot of it is you've got to tailor to people's needs. It's alright going, "It's great, I bring out art videos", but if people don't want them then that's bullshit really.

Is there any particular video that you've seen that sticks out for you?

Mal: I don't know, I haven't got a video machine. (laughs)

Back to that old chestnut. When do you want the donation?

Mal: Yeah, I could have a whip round, eh? (laughs) No, seriously video requires a certain amount of discipline that people don't want to give it. And that's fair enough because people don't have time to sit down and watch them – and particularly now they've put 'Night Network' on rather than MTV, so people would far rather sit down and watch that.

Some of the chapters in the previous edition covered your opinions on religion and politics etc. Would you say that your opinions in those areas have changed much?

Mal: No, I don't think my views about those sorts of things have changed. What we've been discussing have been about my personal, local environment, my ambitions and what I see the music as. But on a broader scale I don't think my views on something like politics have changed – apart from becoming a fascist. (laughs) A fascist catholic. (laughs)

But I couldn't really state any particular area or issue where my attitude has changed. I'm still left wing by inclination but not by dogma. I'm still a fucked up catholic same as I was last time. (laughs)

But a vegetarian fucked up catholic.

Mal: Yeah, I suppose that's the only major change. And I still can't work out why I gave up meat, actually. I was with Robin from the Cocteau Twins and we were sat there and for some reason he had a craving for eating a bucket full of Kentucky fried chicken – and he doesn't eat meat either. And I can't work out why I don't eat meat now.

Some people say that it makes them feel healthier.

Mal: Oh God, not when you drink as much as I do! I mean it was never food that made me feel unhealthy. (laughs)

So would still say that you had a pretty hedonistic life-style?

Mal: Oh yeah, I haven't changed in that. The only thing that's changed with me now, is that if I have a really late night or I don't go to bed it takes me a day to get over it – a bit longer to recover.

That's alright I'm safe – as you're older than me.

Mal: But I still do it – that's the point. I still love it. I went to see the Butthole Surfers on friday night and then I went with the Jesus and Mary Chain to a free drinks party and got incredibly drunk.

What are the Jesus and Mary Chain like?

Mal: Oh, they're brilliant. I only really know Jim but he's great. He's a really nice bloke.

Obviously living in London you get more of a chance to meet a lot of other groups.

Mal: Yeah, it's quite funny because the people that I do meet, they're all from outside London and there's this sort of odd camaraderie between all these people who don't come from London and all go out and get drunk.

Presumably when those sort of people get together the last thing they talk about is music.

Mal: Everybody talks about going out, where they live, drinking. You'd be surprised at the people who are a lot more career-minded than I am. Gibby from the Butthole Surfers is a lot sharper than I am – financially – he knows exactly what he's doing. That bloke will make a lot more money than I ever will. And he comes from a lot weirder group than I do. To be honest, meeting people from groups comes a lot less from being in London, 'cos I've been in London for four years, it's come from since I've been a bachelor, or by myself should I say – since Karen and I split up. I suppose that's all it is really – I don't have a girlfriend so I go out more.

Is being unattached a situation you prefer?

Mal: I quite enjoy it actually, I quite enjoy my freedom. Oh God, I hope Karen doesn't read that, she'll kill me! (laughs) Actually Karen and I get on alright – now. (laughs)

Do you think that London night life is up to much?

Mal: I don't know. I don't go out that much. If I do it's just to meet up with friends for a drink. But I don't go out every night – I know

The new look Mallinder - a hint of a smile is indicative of a change in his views on the way the group should be presenting itself.

people who do. Unfortunately, Pete Wylie is a friend of mine, so I don't have a social life I just monitor Wylie's. (laughs)

You've not become paranoid about being a semi-famous person.

Mal: I don't even think about it. I don't think I'm famous at all so it doesn't worry me in the slightest. That's what does worry me – I want to be. (laughs) As I said before I think London's a good ego flattener. Just Like New York – anywhere like that.

What about travel – are there places you'd still like to visit?

Mal: The one place I'd really like to go to that I haven't been is Australia. That's just a fascination in the same way Tokyo and Japan was a few years ago. It is a bit like saying, "been there – done that one – go somewhere else now". (laughs) But the number of places I've been to without working is very very small – and when I have been it has been on package tours.

But you did take your tours quite easily. It was hardly a gig a night stuff.

Mal: Well, yeah that's become the bone of contention between Richard and I really. Because if I'm going to travel and work I'd rather do it intensively and say that's it finished and then take two weeks off and do what I want to do, rather than try and fit it in over a spread out period. You can never really forget you're working – and you're always getting hassled by people.

Although a lot of touring innevitably means a lot of flying. As a fellow hater of flying myself, I can understand Richard not wanting to tour too much.

Mal: The point is I don't knock Richard for not wanting to tour, or not wanting to fly, I don't knock him for not wanting to do those things. But I don't think it should affect myself and what I want to do. That's all it is, really – because I would never want to force him into doing anything. I think quite frankly that doing a tour that was any more than about ten dates would kill Richard – because he's very highly strung in that sense – I can shut off a bit more.

So, tell me about this Father Christmas incident in Milan?

Mal: No, the tape stops now. (laughs) These things are a laugh really, they're not embarrassing at all. Let's face it you'd do it at your own party, or you'd do it at someone else's house for a laugh – so what's the difference. In fact if I could do in public what I do at somebody else's house and it would sell more records, then I'd fucking do it. I don't care.

We've come around to this way of thinking as well just recently about the books we publish.

Mal: I think you've got to be quite frank, nobody particularly wants to read about groups nowadays because most of them are quite boring.

I think that was one of the interesting things about the last book we published, 'Tape Delay', seeing who had something interesting to say and who didn't.

Mal: I think with the areas that book covered it's fair enough, people do want to read about it. But with groups that are more successful, people don't want to read about their pension schemes and things like that.

People would prefer to listen to the records. Mind you, you are probably the exception – people might prefer reading about you than having to listen to your records. (laughs)

Mal: Yeah, I was talking to Amrik earlier in the day and he asked me what I was doing tonight. I told him I was doing an interview with you and he said what for. I told him that you were doing a second edition of the book – I said, "I think they've twigged that we might be splitting up and they're going to cash in on it". Amrik said, "That's great, it's a really good idea – I would do the same thing."

Is there anything you would like to say finally as a coda to the Cabaret Voltaire story?

Mal: Not really, just that it has been good fun so far (pause) – but that's rock 'n' roll! (laughs)

complete
discography

LPs & Cassettes

CABARET VOLTAIRE 1974 - 1976 (cassette IRC 35)

Side One : The Dada Man, Ooraseal, A Sunday Night in Biot, In Quest of the Unusual, Do the Snake, Fade Crisis.
Side Two: Doubled Delivery, Venusian Animals, The Outer Limits, She Loved You.
Recorded at: Chris Watson's loft.
Recorded on: Domestic reel to reel tape recorder.
This cassette is a selection of material recorded during their early formative years of existence. A number of the recordings were part of those which made up the Limited Edition cassette released by Cabaret Voltaire in 1976.

MIX UP (Rough Trade Records. Rough 4)

Side One: Kirlian Photograph, No Escape, Fourth Shot, Heaven and Hell, Eyeless Sight (live 1979).
Side Two: Photophobia, On Every Other Street, Expect Nothing, Capsules.
All tracks - Kirk/Mallinder/Watson except No Escpae (Saxon), Photophobia (words, Victor).
Chris Watson: Electronics, Tapes.
Richard H. Kirk: Guitar, Wind instruments.
Stephen Mallinder: Bass, Vocals.
with
Haydn Bois-Weston: Drums.
Recorded at: Western Works July/Aug 1979.
Produced by: Cabaret Voltaire.
Sleeve by: Cabaret Voltaire.

LIVE AT THE YMCA (Rough Trade Records.)

Side One: Untitled, On Every Other Street, Nag Nag Nag, The Set Up.
Side Two: Expect Nothing, Havoc, Here She Comes Now, No Escape, Baader Meinhof.
Recorded at: YMCA London, October 1979.

THE VOICE OF AMERICA (Rough Trade Records. Rough 11)

Side One: The Voice of America/The Damage is Done, Partially submerged, Kneel to the Boss, Premonition.
Side Two: This is Entertainment, If the Shadows Could March? (1974), Stay Out of It, Obsession, News From Nowhere, Messages Received.
All Tracks Kirk/Mallinder/Watson.
Chris Watson: Electronics, Tapes.
Richard H. Kirk: Guitar, Wind instruments.
Stephen Mallinder: Bass, Electronic percussion, Vocals.
with
Haydn Bois-Weston: Drums.
Recorded at: Western Works Mar/Apr 1980.
Produced by: Cabaret Voltaire.
Sleeve by: Cabaret Voltaire.

LIVE AT THE LYCEUM (Rough Trade Tapes. Copy 002)

Side One: Taxi Music/Seconds Too Late, Your Agent Man, Untitled, Sluggin' Fer Jesus.
Side Two: Kneel to the Boss, Obsession, A Thousand Ways.
All Tracks Kirk/Mallinder/Watson.
Chris Watson: Keyboards, Synthesisors, Tapes.
Richard H. Kirk: Guitar, Wind instruments.
Stephen Mallinder: Bass, Percussion, Vocals.
Recorded at: The Lyceum, London, on February 8th 1981.

RED MECCA (Rough Trade Records. Rough 27)

Side One: A Touch of Evil, Sly Doubt, Landslide, A Thousand Ways.
Side Two: Red Mask, Split-second Feeling, Black Mask, Spread the Virus, A Touch of Evil (reprise).
All Tracks Kirk/Mallinder/Watson.
Chris Watson: Vox Continental, Tapes.
Richard H. Kirk: Synthesisor, Guitar, Clarinet, Horns, Strings.
Stephen Mallinder: Bass, Vocals, Guitars, Bongos.
Recorded at: Western Works, May 1981.
Produced by: Cabaret Voltaire.
Sleeve by: Neville Brody/Cabaret Voltaire.

2 x 45 (Rough Trade Records. Rough 42)

Record One:
Side One: Breathe Deep, Yashar.
Side Two: Protection.
Chris Watson: Vox Continental, Tapes.
Richard H. Kirk: Synthesisor, Guitar, Clarinet, Saxophone.
Stephen Mallinder: Bass, Vocals, Percussion.
Recorded at: Western Works, October 1981.
Produced by: Cabaret Voltaire.
Record Two:
Side One: War of Nerves (TES), Wait and Shuffle.
Side Two: Get Out of My Face.
Richard H. Kirk: Guitar, Sax, Roland SH09 and CSQ 100, Tapes.
Stephen Mallinder: Bass, Vocals, Tapes.
with
Nort: Drums and Percussion.
Eric Random: Guitar and Percussion.
Recorded at: Pluto Studios, Manchester, February 1982.
Produced by: Cabaret Voltaire/Phil Bush.
Sleeve By: Neville Brody/Cabaret Voltaire.

THE PRESSURE COMPANY - BENEFIT FOR SOLIDARITY (Solid No 1)

Side One: War of Nerves, Wait and Shuffle.
Side Two: Get Out of My Face, Vitreous China.
Recorded at: Sheffield University (live), 19th Jan 1982.
The Pressure Company were: Richard H. Kirk, Stephen Mallinder, Eric Random.

HAI! (Rough Trade Records. RTD1)

Side One: Walls of Kyoto, 3 Days Monk, Yashar (version).
Side Two: Over and Over, Diskono, Taxi Music.
Richard H. Kirk: Guitar, Clarinet, Synthesisor, Tapes.
Stephen Mallinder: Bass, Vocals, Tapes.
with
Alan Fish: Drums, Percussion.
Recorded at: Tsubaki House (live), Tokyo, March 23 1982.
Produced by: Cabaret Voltaire.
Sleeve and photos: G. house, Richard H. Kirk, Chataru Mogi.

JOHNNY YESNO SOUNDTRACK (Doublevision DVR1)

Side One: Taxi Music, Hallucination Sequence, DT's, Cold Turkey.
Side Two: The Quarry (In the Wilderness), Title Sequence, Taxi Music (dub).
Recorded at: Western Works, June 1981.
Produced by: Kirk/Mallinder/Watson.
Sleeve by: Neville Brody.

THE CRACKDOWN (Some Bizarre/Virgin CV1)

Side One: 24 - 24, In the Shadows, Talking Time, Animation.
Side Two: Over and Over, Just Fascination, Why Kill Time (When you Can Kill Yourself), Haiti, Crackdown.
Richard H. Kirk: Synthesisors, Sequencers, Guitar, Sax, Shakahachi, Grand Piano.
Stephen Mallinder: Bass, Vocals, Trumpet, Grand Piano.
with
Alan Fish: Drums, Percussion.
Dave Ball: Keyboard rhythm assistance.
Recorded at: Trident Studios, London, December 1982.
Produced by: Cabaret Voltaire/Flood.
Sleeve by: Phil Barnes/Neville Brody/Ken Prust.
Early copies contained a limited edition 12" EP (CVDV1) containing four tracks from the Doublevision video. These tracks later appeared as extra tracks on the Compact Disc.
Side One: Diskono, Doublevision.
Side Two: Moscow, Badge of Evil.
Recorded at: Western Works.
Produced by: Cabaret Voltaire.

MICRO-PHONIES (Some Bizarre/Virgin CV2)

Side One: Do Right, The Operative, Digital Rasta, Spies in the Wires, Theme from Earthshaker.
Side Two: James Brown, Slammer, Blue Heat, Sensoria.
Richard H. Kirk: Guitar, Wind instruments, Synthesisor, Fairlight.
Stephen Mallinder: Bass, Vocals.
with
Roger Quail: Drums, Percussion.
Mark Tattersall: Percussion.

Eric Random: Tablas.
Recorded at: Western Works.
Produced by: Flood/Cabaret Voltaire.
Mixed at: Sarm West.
Sleeve: Phil Barnes/Neville Brody.

DRINKING GASOLINE (Some Bizarre/Virgin CVM 1. Double 12")

Side One: Kino
Side Two: Sleepwalking
Side Three: Big Funk
Side Four: Ghostalk
Recorded at: Western Works, Dec '84 - Jan '85.
Produced by: Cabaret Voltaire.
Drums: Mark Tattersall (Kino/Sleepwalking).
Sleeve Graphics: Paul White.

THE COVENANT, THE SWORD AND THE ARM OF THE LORD (Some Bizarre/Virgin)

Side One: L21ST, I Want You, Hell's Home, Kickback, The Arm of the Lord.
Side Two: Warm, Golden Halos, Motion Rotation, Whip Blow, The Web.
Recorded at: Western Works
Produced by: Cabaret Voltaire
Sleeve by: Neville Brody

THE GOLDEN MOMENTS OF CABARET VOLTAIRE (Rough Trade. CD only)

Track listing: Do the Mussolini, Nag Nag Nag, Photophobia, Expect Nothing, Seconds Too Late, This is Entertainment, Obsession, Sluggin' Fer Jesus, Landslide, Red Mask, Get Out of My Face.
Sleeve: Neville Brody

EIGHT CREPESCULE TRACKS

Side One: Sluggin' Fer Jesus (Part One), Sluggin' Fer Jesus (Part Two), Fool's Game, Yashar.
Side Two: Your Agent Man, Gut Level, Invocation, Theme From Shaft.
Recorded at: Western Works
Produced by: Cabaret Voltaire

CODE (EMI PCS 7312)

Side One: Don't Argue, Sex/Money/Freaks, Thank You America, Here To Go.
Side Two: Trouble (Won't Stop), White Car, No one Here, Life Slips By, Code.
Recorded at: Love Street Studios
Produced by: Adrian Sherwood/Cabaret Voltaire
Sleeve by: Neville Brody/Cornel Windlin.

7" & 12" SINGLES

EXTENDED PLAY (Rough Trade. RT 003)

A Side: Talk Over, Here She Comes Now (Reed)
B Side: Do The Mussolini Headkick, The Set Up
Recorded at: Western Works, 1978.
Produced by: Cabaret Voltaire.

NAG NAG NAG (Rough Trade. RT018)

A Side: Nag Nag Nag
B Side: Is That Me (Finding Someone at the Door Again)?
Recorded at: A) Western Works B) Live 1975.
Produced by: Geoff Travis and Mayo Thompson.
Sleeve: Cabaret Voltaire (Photos live at Gibus Club, Paris by Richard Waters.

SILENT COMMAND (Rough Trade. RT 035)

A Side: Silent Command
B Side: Chance versus Causality
Recorded at: Western Works, October 1979.
Produced by: Cabaret Voltaire.
Sleeve: Cabaret Voltaire.

THREE MANTRAS (Rough Trade. RT 038 - Available as 12" only)

A Side: Western Mantra
B Side: Eastern Mantra
Recorded at: Western Works, January 1980.
Produced by: Cabaret Voltaire.
John Clayton: Additional percussion on Eastern Mantra.
Jane: Jerusalem market tapes on Eastern Mantra.

EDDIES OUT/WALLS OF JERICHO (Rough Trade. RT 096 - Available as 12" only)

A Side: Eddies Out
B Side: Walls of Jericho
Recorded at: Western Works, July 1981.
Produced by: Cabaret Voltaire.
Sleeve Photos: Anton Corbijn.
Early copies contained a limited edition 7" single
A Side: Jazz the Glass
B Side: Burnt to the Ground

SECONDS TOO LATE (Rough Trade. RT 060)

A Side: Seconds Too Late
B Side: Control Addict
Recorded at: Western Works, September 1981.
Produced by: Cabaret Voltaire and Geoff Travis.
Sleeve: Cabaret Voltaire.

SLUGGIN' FER JESUS (Les Disques Du Crepescule. TW 120)

A Side: Sluggin' Fer Jesus (Part One)
B Side: Your Agent Man, Sluggin' Fer Jesus (Part Two)
Recorded at: Western Works, 1981.
Produced by: Cabaret Voltaire.
Sleeve: Neville Brody.

FOOL'S GAME (Les Disques Du Crepescule. TW 120)

A Side: Fool's Game
B Side: Gut Level (Sluggin' Fer Jesus, Part Three)
Recorded at: Western Works, 1981.
Produced by: Cabaret Voltaire.

YASHAR (Factory Benelux/Factory New York. FBN 25)

A Side: Yashar
B Side: Yashar
Recorded at: Western Works.
Remixed by: John Robie in New York.
Sleeve: Patrick Roques.

CRACKDOWN/JUST FASCINATION (Some Bizarre/Virgin CVS1-12)

A Side: Crackdown
B Side: Just Fascination
On the 7" single the A and B Sides were reversed.
Recorded at: Trident Studios, London.
Produced by: John Luongo assisted by Cabaret Voltaire.

THE DREAM TICKET (Some Bizzare/Virgin CVS2-12)

A Side: The Dream Ticket
B Side: Safety Zone
Recorded at: A) Trident Studios, London. B) Western Works.
Produced by: A) Cabaret Voltaire and Flood. B) Cabaret Voltaire.

SENSORIA (Some Bizarre/Virgin CVS 3-12)

A Side: Sensoria
B Side: Cut the Damn Camera
Recorded at: Western Works (Remixed at Sarm West).
Produced by: John 'Tokes' Potoker with Cabaret Voltaire.
Sleeve by: Ian Wright.

JAMES BROWN (Some Bizarre/Virgin CVS 4-12)

A Side: James Brown
B Side: Bad Self Part 1
Recorded at: Western Works
Produced by:Cabaret Voltaire/John 'Tokes' Potoker
Sleeve by: Neville Brody

I WANT YOU (Some Bizarre/Virgin CVS 5-12)

A Side: I Want You
B Side: Drink Your Poison, C.O.M.A.
Recorded at: Western Works
Produced by: Cabaret Voltaire
Sleeve by: Neville Brody

THE DRAIN TRAIN (Doublevision DVR 21)

A Side: (Shakedown) The Whole Thing
B Side: Menace, Electro-motive
Contained extra 12" of (Shakedown) Version and (Shakedown) Dub
Recorded at: Western Works, March 1986.
Produced by: Cabaret Voltaire.
Sleeve by: Joe Ewart.

DON'T ARGUE

A Side: Don't Argue
B Side: Don't Argue (Hate and Destroy mix)
Recorded at: Love Street Studios
Produced by: Adrian Sherwood, remixed by John Robie/Cabaret Voltaire
Sleeve by: Neville Brody

HERE TO GO

A Side: Here To Go
B Side: Here To Go (Space Dub)
Recorded at: Love Street Studios
Produced by: Adrian Sherwood/Cabaret Voltaire
Sleeve by: Neville Brody/Cornel Windlin

SOLO PROJECTS BY RICHARD H. KIRK

DISPOSABLE HALF-TRUTHS (Industrial cassette IRC 34)

Side One: Synthesthia, Outburst, Information Therapy, Magic Words, Command, Thermal Damage.
Side Two: Plate Glass Replicas, Insect Friends of Allah, Scatalist, False Erotic Love, LD 50, LD 60, Amnesic Dislocation.
Recorded at: Western Works, 1980.
Produced by: Richard H. Kirk.
Lyn: Clarinet, guitar and voices on some tracks.
The cassette was accompanied by a photocopied hand-out.

TIME HIGH FICTION (Doublevision. DVR 2)

Record One
Side One: The Greedy Eye, Shaking Down the Tower of Babel, Force of Habit, Day of Waiting.
Side Two: Black Honeymoon, Nocturnal Children, Wire trap, The Power of Autosuggestion.
Record Two
Side One: Dead Relatives Part One
Side Two: Dead Relatives Part Two
Recorded at: Western Works, October 1979 - April 1982.
Produced by: Richard H. Kirk
Sleeve: Phil Barnes

LEATHER HANDS - Richard H. Kirk/Pete Hope (Doublevision 12". DVR 15)

A Side: Leather Hands (Master Mix)
B Side: Leather Hands (Radio Mix) Leather Hands (Crash Mix)
Recorded at: Western Works, May 1985.
Produced by: Richard H. Kirk
Sleeve: Phil Barnes/Naked Art

HIPNOTIC (Rough Trade 12". RTT 199)

A Side: Hipnotic
B Side: Martyrs of Palestine
Recorded at: Western Works, April 1986.
Produced by: Richard H. Kirk
Sleeve: Phil Barnes & Richard H. Kirk/Naked Art

HOODOO TALK - LP Richard H. Kirk/Pete Hope (NTV LP 28)

Side One: Intro, Numb Skull, N.O., Cop Out.
Side Two: Surgeons, 50 Tears, Leather Hands, 50 Tears (reprise).
Recorded at: Western Works
Produced by: Richard H. Kirk

BLACK JESUS VOICE (Rough 99)

Side One: Street Gang (it really hurts), Hipnotic, Boom Sha La.
Side Two: Black Jesus Voice, Martyrs of Palestine, This is the H Bomb Sound,
Shortwave.
Recorded at: Western Works 1986
Produced by: Richard H. Kirk.
Sleeve by: Phil Barnes/R.H. Kirk

UGLY SPIRIT (RTM 189)

Side One: The Emperor, Confessions, Infantile, Frankie Machine (part one).
Side Two: Hollywood Babylon, Thai, Voodoo, Frankie Machine (part two).
Recorded at: Western Works 1986
Produced by: Richard H. Kirk
Sleeve by: Phil Barnes/R.H. Kirk

SURGEONS (12" Single) - Richard H. Kirk/Pete Hope

A Side: Surgeons (Remix)
B Side: N.O.

LET'S GET DOWN by Wicky Wacky (12" Single) As yet unreleased.

A Side: Let's Get Down
B Side: (Unknown at time of publication)
Richard H. Kirk under the name Wicky Wacky

SOLO PROJECTS - STEPHEN MALLINDER

TEMPERATURE DROP (Fetish 12". FE 12)

A Side: Temperature Drop
B Side: Cool Down
Recorded at: Western Works, 1981
Produced by: Stephen Mallinder
Sleeve by: Neville Brody

POW WOW (Fetish LP. FM 2010) (re-released by Doublevision. DVR 16)

Side One: The Devil in Me, 0.58, Pow Wow, Three piece Swing, 1.20
Side Two: 1.37, In Smoke, 1.59, Length of Time, 1.34
Recorded at: Western Works
Produced by: Stephen Mallinder
Sleeve by: Neville Brody

GALAXY by Love Street (EMI 12" Single)

A Side: Galaxy
B Side: Come On Down to Love Street
Love Street were Stephen Mallinder/Dave Ball/Robert Gordon
Recorded at: Fon Studios
Produced by: Fon Force
Sleeve by: Designer's Republic

CABARET VOLTAIRE TRACKS INCLUDED ON COMPILATIONS

FACTORY SAMPLER EP (FAC 4)

Tracks: Baader Meinhof, Sex in Secret

BUSINESS UNUSUAL (Cherry Red ARED 2)

Track: Do the Mussolini Headkick

WANNA BUY A BRIDGE (Rough US 3)

Track: Nag Nag Nag

NME/ROUGH TRADE CASSETTE (Copy 001)

Track: Raising the Count

THE FACTORY COMPILATION (Facbn 7)

Tracks: No Escape, Sluggin' Fer Jesus

A DAY IN OCTOBER (Les Disques Du Crepescule)

Track: Your Agent Man

CHANTONS NOEL - THE GHOSTS OF CHRISTMAS PAST (Crepescule TW1 058)

Track: Invocation

VINYL MAGAZINE #13 (Free Flexi-disc)

Track: Over and Over

NME MIGHTY REEL Cassette (NME 004)

Track: Loosen the Clamp

INDUSTRIAL RECORDS STORY (Illuminated Records JAMS 39)

Track: A Saturday Night in Biot

NME RAGING SPOOL Cassette

Track: Mercy Man

IF YOU CAN'T PLEASE YOURSELF, YOU CAN'T PLEASE YOUR SOUL - Some Bizarre

Track: Product Patrol

DIAMOND IN THE MOUTH OF A CORPSE

Track: Dead Man's Shoes
Lp featuring Burroughs/Giorno/Nick Cave and others

SALVATION (Soundtrack to the Movie) (TWI 774)

Tracks: Twanky Party, Jesus Saves.

CLEAN, BUT IT JUST LOOKS DIRTY

Track: Trust in the Lord
Video compilation by John Giorno (Video Pack 3)

DOUBLEVISION CATALOGUE

RECORDS

DVR 1   JOHNNY YESNO SOUNDTRACK - Cabaret Voltaire - LP

DVR 2   TIME HIGH FICTION - Richard H. Kirk - LP x 2

DVR 3   ELEMANTAL 7 - CTI - LP

DVR 4   "BANG" - AN OPEN LETTER - The Hafler Trio - LP

DVR 5   IN LIMBO - Lydia Lunch - LP (Now WSP 6)

DVR 6   OUT OF THE FLESH - Chakk - 12" Single

DVR 7   MAD AS MANKIND - Eric Random and the Bedlamites - 12" Single

DVR 8   EUROPEAN RENDEVOUS - CTI - LP

DVR 9   PLAYS "KICKABYE" - Annie Hogan - Mini LP

DVR 10 MUSCLE IN - The Box - EP

DVR 11 TIME-SPLICE - Eric Random and the Bedlamites - LP

DVR 12 Aborted

DVR 13 SKIN SCRAPED BACK - Workforce - 12" Single

DVR 14 ONE-TWO PUNCH - Don King - Mini LP

DVR 15 LEATHER HANDS - Pete Hope/Richard H. Kirk - 12" Single

DVR 16 POW WOW PLUS - Stephen Mallinder - LP

DVR 17 MOLE SHOW/VILENESS FATS - The Residents - LP

DVR 18 4 HOURS - Clock DVA - 12" Single

DVR 19 THIRST - Clock DVA - LP

DVR 20 SPECTRUM TEST - Various - Double LP

DVR 21 THE DRAIN TRAIN - Cabaret Voltaire - 12" Single

DOUBLEVISION VIDEOS

DV1 DOUBLE VISION PRESENTS - Cabaret Voltaire - 90 mins

DV2 HEATHEN EARTH/LIVE AT OUNDLE SCHOOL - Throbbing Gristle - 120 mins

DV3 JOHNNY YESNO - Pete Care/Cabaret Voltaire - 58 mins

DV4 TV WIPEOUT (VIDEO MAGAZINE) - Various - 110 mins

DV5 ELEMENTAL 7 - CTI - 58 mins

DV6 7 SONGS/TRANQULISER - 23 Skidoo - 58 mins

DV7 IN THE SHADOW OF THE SUN - Derek Jarman/TG - 58 mins

DV8 EUROPEAN RENDEVOUS - CTI - 50 mins

DV9 MOLESHOW/VILENESS FATS - The Residents - 60 mins

DV10 GHOST SONATA - Tuxedo Moon - 60 mins

WDV1 GASOLINE IN YOUR EYE - Cabaret Voltaire - 82 mins

books
films
music

SELECTED READING

DADA MANIFESTOS
POPISM by Andy Warhol
FROM A TO B AND BACK AGAIN by Andy Warhol
THE THIRD MIND by William Burroughs and Brion Gysin
NAKED LUNCH by Willaim Burroughs
THE JOB, THE ELECTRONIC REVOLUTION by William Burroughs
WITH WILLIAM BURROUGHS by Victor Bockris
MY LAST BREATH by Luis Bunuel
NEW SOVIET PSYCHIC DISCOVERIES by Gris and Dick
ELECTRIC COOL AID ACID TEST by T. Wolfe
LAST EXIT TO BROOKLYN by Hubert Selby Jnr.
CONFESSIONS OF ALEISTER CROWLEY by Aleister Crowley
THE ATROCITY EXHIBITION by J.G. Ballard
UNLIMITED DREAM COMPANY by J.G. Ballard
A SCANNER DARKLY by Phillip K. Dick
HEAVEN AND HELL/THE DOORS OF PERCEPTION by Aldous Huxley
MARQUIS DE SADE by Iwan Bloch
JUSTINE by Marquis De Sade
VENUS IN FURS by Masoch
INDUSTRIAL CULTURE HANDBOOK by Re Search Magazine (features Cabaret
Voltaire amongst others)

SELECTED VIEWING

ALL BUNUEL FILMS
ALL WARHOL/MORRISEY FILMS
ALL FELLINI FILMS
ALL ANTHONY BALCH FILMS
ALL DEREK JARMAN FILMS
ALL KENNETH ANGER FILMS

A TOUCH OF EVIL - Orson Welles
THE REBEL - Robert Day (starring Tony Hancock)
APOCALYPSE NOW - Francis Ford Coppola
TAXI DRIVER - Martin Scorcese
THE MAN WITH THE GOLDEN ARM - Otto Preminger (starring Frank Sinatra)
ENTER THE DRAGON - Robert Clouse (starring Bruce Lee)
MAD MAX 1 & 2 - George Miller
EMPIRE OF THE SENSES - Oshima
CLOCKWORK ORANGE - Kubrick
PSYCHO - Hitchcock
TEXAS CHAINSAW MASSACRE - Tobe Hooper
REPULSION - Roman Polanski
THE OUTER LIMITS - '60s TV Sci fi series
SWEDISH EROTICA
NUMEROUS HORROR MOVIES
WAR/RIOT/TORTURE/NAZI film footage

SELECTED LISTENING

JAMES BROWN
MILES DAVIS
JUNIOR WALKER
VELVET UNDERGROUND
NICO
KRAFTWERK
CAN/HOLGER CZUKAY
NEU
YELLO
Early ROXY MUSIC
ENO
THE RESIDENTS
THROBBING GRISTLE
NON
TEST DEPT.
THE HAFLER TRIO
DIAMANDA GALAS
MARK STEWART AND THE MAFIA
ERIC RANDOM
SUN RA
STEVE REICH
STOCKHAUSEN
IGGY POP/DAVID BOWIE (Low/Heroes/Lust For Life/The Idiot)
NOTHING HERE BUT THE RECORDINGS (William Burroughs LP)
JOHN BARRY
NEW ORDER
EEK-A-MOUSE
DUB REGGAE
TROUBLE FUNK
GO-GO
HOUSE/ACID HOUSE

PHOTOGRAPHIC ACKNOWLEDGEMENTS

N. Arimasa . . . . 67, 107, 117(top), 120(top)

CV Archive 6, 64

P. Carly 44, 55

A. Corbijn 152, 184

P. Cox 167, 192

M. Fish . . . . . 10, 78, 82, 86, 92, 96, 104, 111. (collages)

D. Hallbery . . . . 59, 117(bottom), 138, 161

M. Lebon 197

NME 72

Music Maker 127

Sounds 130

G. Spiers 156, 170

Photographs not credited were unknown at the time of publication. Anyone concerned can contact the publisher and a credit will be included in future editions.

Thanks also to:

Richard and Mal for access to archive material

Paul Smith (Doublevision)

Hannah Eichler (EMI)

TAPE DELAY by Charles Neal (ISBN 0 946719 02 0)

Tape Delay is a book that reflects the initiatives of those who have deviated from the mainstream in sound, word and image since the mid-seventies. Comprising mainly of interview material, the author has also collected a wide variety of original material from many of the book's contributors ranging from prose pieces to illustrations and photographs.

Extensively illustrated, the book consists of 256 pages that provide the first comprehensive focus for the undercurrents that still exert a strong influence on the 'music industry'.

Full list of contributors in alphabetical order are: Marc Almond, Dave Ball, Cabaret Voltaire, Nick Cave, Chris & Cosey, Coil, Einsturzende Neubauten, Diamanda Galas, Genesis P-Orridge, Michael Gira, The Hafler Trio, Laibach, Lydia Lunch, Matt Johnson, New Order, Psychic TV, Boyd Rice, Henry Rollins, Clint Ruin, Mark E. Smith, Sonic Youth, Stevo, Mark Stewart, Swans, Test Dept, David Tibet, Touch.

Price £8.95 (add £1.00 UK, £1.50 Europe, £2.00p Worldwide for postage).

EVERY SECOND COUNTS by Ari Vatanen (ISBN 0 946719 04 7)

This colourful biography covers Finnish former World Rally Champion Ari Vatanen's full career since he started rallying in 1971. He describes, together with journalist Vesa Vaisanen, his love of driving and many of the aspects that make car rallying the unique sport it is. But it is also a very personal story which covers his difficult return to the wheel after the accident in Argentina which nearly killed him in 1985. It was an accident which was to leave him, not only with serious injuries, but also with a long harrowing depression which included a fear that he had contracted AIDS.

Already a best seller in Finland and France, this English language edition is fully updated, including his return to the victory rostrum in the Paris-Dakar Rally in 1987, and the controversy surrounding his car in the same rally in 1988. The book contains 296 pages and many photos (in colour and black & white) and is not only an essential guide to anyone who is interested in rallying, but also a moving account of someone reconciling a return to a dangerous sport, and of a fight back to fitness after serious injury and depression.

Price £7.95 (add £1.00 UK, £1.50 Europe, £2.00p Worldwide for postage).

THE MOMENT SPLICE EXPERIMENTS by B.J. Morrison (ISBN 0 946719 004)

Originally published in 1983 and thought to be out of print - a limited edition of 300 copies has been found during an SAF reorganisation.
This unique 32 page melding of words and photographs represents the concentrated mind of this obscurist poetrician and English language semiologist who was last reported to be living in Kuala Lumpar.

Price £2.00 (UK) £2.50 (Europe) £3.00 (Rest of the World) Prices include P&P.

ORDERING DETAILS.

Please send orders to the following address:

SAF Publishing Ltd. PO Box 151,
Harrow, Middx. HA3 0DH England.

To order any of these titles by credit card (Access or Visa)
Telephone: 01 904 6263 (Mon-Fri, 9.00 am - 5.00 pm)
All cheques / IMO's must be made payable to SAF in pounds sterling.